# TRACES OF A BOY

## Reflections of the Unfathomable

RUSS GRABB

Traces of a Boy
Copyright © 2023 by Russ Grabb

Tellwell Talent
www.tellwell.ca

ISBN
978-1-77941-007-8 (Hardcover)
978-1-77941-006-1 (Paperback)
978-1-77941-008-5 (eBook)

"I write entirely to find out what I'm thinking, what I'm looking at, what I see and what it means—and what I want and what I fear."

— Joan Didion, 1970s pioneer of creative nonfiction

## Author in Brief:

Born in Toronto in 1957, Russ is a retired business consultant and former superintendent with the Royal Canadian Mounted Police (RCMP). The father of two adoring daughters, Megan and Alena, and the paternal grandson of Russian immigrants, he currently resides in North Vancouver, Canada with his loving spouse, Marianne. Diagnosed in 2020 with a rare form of incurable leukemia cancer, he has a truly astonishing story to share. Every single word of what he has to say is verifiably true and accurate.

## In Dedication:

This out-loud-narration diary is dedicated to Stephanie Steele. She emerged as the first person outside my own household to help guide me through the complexities of this healing journey. Without her kindness and devotion to defending the truth, there would be no jaw-dropping tale of cruelty to share with the world.

# PART I:

When a precious little one dies
right before our eyes ...

# CHAPTER 1: As Bequeathed

ERNEST HEMINGWAY once said that the best place to begin writing any book about yourself is to first write down one true sentence—the absolutely truest sentence that comes to mind. Journalists always remind us to never bury the lead—and to always make sure the first phrase of any disclosure of truth stands as the most astonishing thing one could ever say about it. I know this because they've been scolding me on this moronic point for years. I'm no expert over here, but I would have to say the truest thing I could ever say about myself is probably the reality that because I had been so badly beaten and violated as a child, my entire life became not much more than a desperate quest for safety and inner peace that frankly didn't go so well. It defined who I was as a person for well over 60 years. It was made even worse by an equally harmful blanket of elaborate self-deception. It meant I never really got a chance to live out my mischief-making adolescence until I was well into my early twenties. As I recall, it was a period of unbridled excess. It was the late 1970s, early 1980s. Everywhere you went folks were getting high on prurient drugs and espousing the rapturous joy of wild incandescent sex as if we were all still living in the decadent age of Caligula. Armed with the attributes of a grown man—and cursed with what Mr. McConnell said in Grade 5 was my near-Mensa IQ—I was forever being told I carried the impish allure of Richard Gere. However, as I set out to realize my childhood dream of getting married and settling down with a good woman—so we could raise two pigtail-pretty daughters on some quiet hobby farm with horses—I remained ever constrained by the mind and maturity of an 8 year old. I soon became a walking-disaster time bomb. It propelled me into no end of chaos, heartache and erotic indulgence. I tried to run. I tried to hide. But I just couldn't seem to shake it. All those dreadful memories of a time when I used to confuse imposed misery with affectionate love continued to seethe and simmer just below the surface.

So, as I toppled into my early thirties I started to think that maybe—just maybe—I might finally be turning some sort of corner. After all, I had just spent the past ten years working as a first-responder constable in what was then considered to be the globally revered RCMP. My duties included patrolling the mean streets of suburban Vancouver in the densely populated neighbourhoods of Burnaby, Richmond and North Vancouver. In the midst of all this big city action there was also that rather entertaining two-year posting to the then newly incorporated Resort Municipality of Whistler. For an adolescent with a gun, it was just so much fun. There were high-speed chases and armed robberies. There were bar fights and barricaded suspects. There were seniors to be helped out of burning apartment buildings. There were old men dying of heart attacks in the parking lot at Zeller's to be resuscitated while weary shoppers stood idle. Of course I'll never forget that time when a hopping mad hashish dealer set my marked police cruiser on fire at 3rd and Chesterfield in June of 1978. There were also all those other occasions when—as a baby-faced rookie—I was asked to assist at the scene of a gory murder, or stand in as a note-taking observer at some gruesome autopsy. Being dispatched to attend the scene of Margaret Trudeau's dinner party at Il Caminetto in Whistler on December 31, 1982—in order to arrest flamboyant oil tycoon J. Bob Carter for causing a ruckus—was just one of the many random encounters I always seemed to have in those days with all the movers and shakers who made up Vancouver's corrupt power elite, then known as the Heathens of Howe Street. When they weren't buying and selling professional sport franchises—and hawking fraudulent stock options out on the trading floor of the VSE—they were busy outdoing the likes of Mötely Crüe by knocking back poppers and getting steak sandwiches and lunchtime blowjobs from coked out strippers at the Marble Arch. Word on the street at the time was that this Carter fuck was also a child rapist with a proclivity for girls in Grade 9. Best-selling author Joseph Wambaugh would have stood in awe at what I got to see. In my twenties, I became the very epitome of his archetypal protagonist: you know, that flawed beat cop who flirts with danger and dysfunction, whose ethos pulls back the curtain on human frailty—and unearths the gritty texture of urban policework in a barren world that has no shame and shows no mercy. It all came to a crescendo of boiling intrigue when I learned that the wooden crate of M-16 rifles for which I had to help prepare all the approval permits at the front counter of North Vancouver RCMP Detachment in 1981—for the filming of some low-budget flick called *First Blood*—had been stolen on set by a sketchy trio of local army reservists looking to create righteous mayhem on the streets of Vancouver.

As the cocaine-soaked disco era started to wind down, I lost count how many times the likes of a married women from the tony British Properties—racing her candy apple red 450SL convertible down Lonsdale—would pull over at the first sign of my speed trap incitement, tilt back her Vuarnet sunglasses with a sassy Farrah Fawcett smile, and quip, "How about lunch sometime, handsome? I'm thinking the Attic at Park Royal? You know I love my husband, darlin, but this is just something I need." So, between the exhilaration of street policing, and the alluring charm of sexual cannibalism in the golden age of fondue parties and chocolate brown kitchen appliances from Eaton's, it was just one endless stream of ill-gotten fodder for me to keep weaving even more layers of the shaky embroidered truth I was then using to evade my past—and search for that eviscerated little scamp who drowned and went missing in 1965.

By the time I cascaded headlong into my early forties I had become pretty darn adept at putting my constructed reality into high gear. In my mind I nurtured this silly notion that I was unstoppable—that the universe was a perfect place within which nobody ever got hurt. Onto other people I projected noble qualities and degrees of beauty that did not actually exist. Through my actions I left the world with the completely false impression I was unusually gifted and emotionally intelligent. It was all made possible by the fact that years earlier, at age 30, I had been transferred out of my uniform patrolman duties by the RCMP, in order to work in a wide range of major crime investigation settings across the Force. Given my acquired expertise with helping to solve cold case murders, it wasn't long before I was also being asked to briefly take over as the lead television spokesperson for the RCMP for the entire Province of British Columbia. As an unaccompanied minor with an Armani suit and a shoulder holster, it was once again totally cool fun. I felt like a cancer survivor from the pediatric ward being flown to Disneyland by the Children's Wish Foundation to meet Minnie Mouse. Imagining I was Sonny Crockett from *Miami Vice*, my many detective assignments took me to every corner of Canada, stateside to big cities like Boston and Detroit, and all across the world to exotic places such as NATO headquarters in Belgium, the jungles of the Philippines, and the Canadian embassy on Kostolna Street in Kyiv. Helping detectives from Saanich PD crack the Marguerite Telesford murder case over on Vancouver Island still stands as one of the more memorable moments of this mind-blowing chapter of my life. It was all just one colossal blur of blood-soaked crime scenes, spine-chilling interviews with incarcerated serial killers, high-risk takedowns of violent offenders, cheeky kibitzing with prosecutors Austin Cullen and Mike Hicks over the wording of wiretap affidavits, split-screen interviews with Peter Mansbridge, and long boring waits at Gate 22, Heathrow. Hell, there was even that time when I was shipped off to Lyon, France to investigate a leak of secret intel from Interpol regarding a CIA-monitored Russian oligarch. It was that time when I was assigned to look into the questionable conduct of one of the highest-ranking FBI agents posted over in Europe. It kinda felt like being dragged down into the plot of some elaborate Robert Ludlum novel. It was a case that captured huge media attention after a Siberian penal colony survivor—who *Time* magazine once described as the most pernicious unindicted criminal in the world—successfully sued *The London Times* for falsely connecting him to the $10 billion money laundering scandal over at the Bank of New York. Always looking to see just how far Sonny Crockett might get on some alluring overseas assignment, my mission was to figure out what role that FBI agent might have played in helping this iconic newspaper get their facts so terribly wrong about suspected nuclear arms smuggler, Grigori Loutchansky. Boy, you should have seen the signs of relief in Washington when I was able to clear her of any wrongdoing after making inquiries all over Europe and spending two intense weeks in Lyon. I didn't get a call from Mike Wallace and *60 Minutes*, but it was clear from all the back-channel chatter I heard that having interviewed this Russian fat cat in 1998, Mike still had questions as to why the DNC would invite him to dine at a black-tie fundraiser with President Bill Clinton back in 1993. No truth to the rumour yellowcake from Kazakhstan had been featured on the dessert menu.

So while all my many major crime investigation peers derived great personal reward from solving serious crimes, I derived great existential survival escapism from all the glamour, travel and television news exposure. At the back of my mind was always this searing fear that if I got too close to the notion of bringing closure and resolution for grieving families, I too might have to confront all the many acts of brutality and sexual defilement that had been so cruelly beset upon me, way back in the 1960s. Hiding behind contrived adulation and hunter green Gordon Gekko suspenders just seemed like a smarter play for me.

Luckily, embedded deep into the fabric of all this crazy intrigue was a gentle nurturing thread of wholesome benevolence. It was that good woman I'd been dreaming of since, well, since forever. She was my true earth angel. She was Marianne Bianco from Peterborough. She came into my life around the time I was making that big transition from street cop to major crime detective. We very soon got married close to where we first met up in Whistler. We never did settle down on that hobby farm, but it didn't take us long to find our collective voice and build one hell of a happy home out in the clamour-free burbs. Soon came our firstborn child, Megan. Not long thereafter, our youngest, Alena. Although I did my best to insulate them from all the stressors of my job, all three ended up playing a prominent supporting actress role in the tragic comedy that was my batshit crazy career in the RCMP.

I'm sure for Marianne her most unforgettable anecdote would be that time when I was out of town on a big case and a disheveled 20-year-old heroin addict came to our front door at 3:00 a.m., claiming she worked for me as an informant, asking if I could give her a big hug and help her score some molly. For Megan it might be all those times in 1998 when she would ask, "Dad, if you used to be Bob Paulson's boss, then why do you hate him so much, and when are you going to put $20 in the swear jar for all those times you say, 'fuck, he pisses me off'?" For Alena it's clearly the fact I missed every single one of her toddler birthday celebrations because I was always being called out to some scene of death. To this day she stills ribs me for walking out on her 6th birthday party because Pierre Elliott Trudeau's young son Michel had died in an avalanche and a French-speaking spokesperson had to go do live hits from the Kootenays for ten days straight. It mattered not to her that the gig also involved me helping to console doe-eyed Sacha and Justin back at the RCMP sub-division headquarters building in Nelson.

So thank God I had Marianne and the girls to keep me grounded—and sensibly focused on mini Polly Pocket dolls, Spice Girl singalongs, and Sunday shopping at Costco. During the brief period when I was the media guy, I lost count how many times a pencil skirt television news reporter—trying her best to be the first to break the 1998 Holtam family massacre story out in Mission—would gingerly approach me after the scrum, and whisper something like, "I'm not a homewrecker, handsome, but I just have to have this story. We can't let that cunt bitch from VU-13 Global be the one. If you can confirm on background Mounties are about to arrest Doug, I'll let you do anything you want to me. Anything. A threesome with what's-her-name from the control room. Anal. Hey, why not just tie me up and money shot me into next July? You just say the good word, Mister." Two journalists who would one day rise to commendable prominence—Jill Bennett and Adrienne Arsenault—weren't among these ravenous predators, but they sure enough stood shoulder to shoulder with them at all the pressers.

So yes, suggesting that a besieged male can actually be centered out for voracious sexual consumption by a predatory female—as if there is such a thing—does indeed sound downright delusional. I can understand why so many people would consider it just another chauvinistic ploy to shamelessly portray oneself as a sensitive ladies' man who's good in bed. But for me, it's just how it's always been. I've never known anything different. It all started in earnest on December 28, 1960, in a tiny family bungalow on Brampton Road in suburban Etobicoke, on the western edge of what is now the amalgamated City of Toronto. I was 3. It was when I first started to talk and express ideas. And boy, did I ever have ideas—precocious ideas that would surely disrupt the orchestrated reality of any personality disordered parent. It carried on with oscillating intensity for 11 more years in the sleepy, pleasantville cities of Drummondville and Bramalea. It tapered off when my family relocated to Guildwood Village in Scarborough in the summer of 1971—around the time I was just going into Grade 9, and America was ramping up combat action in Vietnam.

It was also just a few months after that long drawn out debate over Pierre Elliot Trudeau's battle cry "just watch me" inspired me to adopt my own "war measures" footing—and start fighting back with a vengeance. I'm thinking one day Alena will come to accept that my failure to stick around and watch her blow out those six candles was more than just me being blindly fixated on my career. Going on national television for two weeks in order to offer a calm, reassuring voice—and timely updates—to a heartbroken and bedridden former prime minister back in Montreal was just something that I felt very obligated to do.

If you're able to keep on listening, you'll soon learn that what happened to me back in the day was real. It's not made up. It's not a ploy. It's not an elaborate yarn being spun by some asshole unable to get beneath ego. It's what actually happened. It robbed me of all hope and dignity. It impregnated me with immense shame and despair. It hurt really bad. It bequeathed to me traits and limitations that would influence every single choice I would later go on to make as an ordinary man in search of an ordinary life. It resurfaced again with earthshattering consequence in my early twenties. It dogged me without mercy well into my late fifties. It's any wonder I'm still alive today to tell you about it. Starting with my unflappable need to dispense out-loud Didionesque narration, you'll forgive me if in doing so I sidestep the dreary industry-standard template for storytelling. Bouncing around from one mesmeric episode to another is just how we unfathomably injured children speak. There are no smooth chapter transitions in our world. There are no opportunities to get beyond the cursory. Those were all stolen from us at a very young age. To obediently follow the tedious rinse-and-repeat publishing stencil that's imposed by all the exalted oracles on high is to reveal that I'm one big fat liar. It's also to reward the very ecosystem of ingrained blindness that I say tried several times to dispatch me straight to a rather untimely and ugly death. As you'll soon see, this is the only reality I've ever known.

**CHAPTER 2:** Four Days in November

WHEN I WOKE UP on the morning of November 1, 2009, it was like any other Sunday, I guess. It was certainly as good a day as any to reflect on where I was with my life. And judging by the opulence of my three-bedroom condominium in Coal Harbour, and the sheen of the fancy Porsche parked downstairs, I was thinking pretty good for a retired RCMP superintendent with no college degree and zero blueblood connections. I was 52 years old. I had been blessed with all this sudden success and elevated wealth, yet something was clearly missing. Then it hit me. It hit me hard. It had been eight years since Marianne and I tragically divorced. She was gone from my life, and I missed her terribly.

For the longest time Marianne and I protested there had been no greener pastures. No falling out of love. No other woman. No how-could-you blame to assign. We both just clung to the factually correct, yet ultimately untrue assertion that it had been a family doctor's failure to correctly diagnose her sudden onset of hypothyroidism that plunged us down a path of slow and painful dissolution. The real truth is that it was all my doing. The whole time, it was me. It all started when I transitioned from jet-setting major crime detective to status-obsessed senior police executive. Saying yes to so many disruptive cross-country transfers and totally unnecessary promotions in rank really didn't help matters much either. With every desperate and dumb career decision that I made we just got farther and farther away from that peaceful hobby farm up on the hill. Ultimately, it was all those national stage call-ups that proved to be our great undoing. First came that special assignment to crack down on criminal malfeasance across the upper chain of command of the Canadian military following that high-profile public inquiry into the repugnant torture of non-combatant civilians by Canadian peacekeepers in Somalia. Embedded directly into the military establishment, I became the first civilian peace officer in the history of the British Commonwealth to possess investigation and charge laying powers that superseded the authority of commanders in the field. I wasn't very popular. I became the target of repeated smear campaigns. It was pretty cool having a green diplomatic passport, but all that transatlantic travel was simply exhausting—and very lonely. I spent so much time at Heathrow airport waiting for connecting flights and shopping for GQ-worthy menswear at Tie Rack I once thought that I might be just some cameo walk-on character from *Love Actually*. Then came that two-year assignment to modernize the atrophied major case management and organized crime curriculum over at the Canadian Police College—one of the lofty duties of which was to give rogatory testimony at the American triple murder trial of Sebastian Burns and Atif Rafay on use of the ever controversial Mr. Big undercover technique across Canada. Then I was tagged to rescue an off-the-rails technology project that was being funded by Parliament to ensure the kind of information sharing snafus that plagued the Paul Bernardo serial killer and Scarborough rapist cases would never happen again. Through it all I kept to myself the coincidence that when I was a teenager growing up in Guildwood Village, in the mid-1970s, my close neighbour was none other than preteen, Paul Bernardo. He lived just three houses away. We both grew up in a middle-class home ruled by a maniacal parent. We both possessed atypical intelligence and athletic promise. We both enjoyed boundless white privilege. We both went to the same venerated high school. One of us grew up to be a serial killer. The other grew up to hunt them down—and to oversee the design of a modern national information system that would make it easier to catch them. The big difference was that he stayed in town and manifested his simmering rage and unbearable rejection in the most sadistic ways imaginable. Having seen the film *Beau Geste* when I was nine years old—about two orphaned boys who join the French Foreign Legion in order to flee their childhood anguish—I fled Scarborough and joined what I thought was going to be the modern Canadian equivalent: the much-celebrated, much-storied Royal Canadian Mounted Police.

Anyway, I finally rounded out my three decade career with the Mounted Madness by perfecting crime reduction models and disaster and pandemic response programs for B.C. in the long arduous lead up to the 2010 Winter Olympics. I'd signed up for the Force in 1977 as a starving architectural sciences student at Ryerson, barely scraping by with no money at age 19. It was when pocket calculators were only just starting to replace old-school slide rules in the physics lab and bellbottoms were still considered fashionable on Saturday night. I retired in 2006 as a net present value millionaire living the high life in downtown Vancouver. I was 49. It was right around that time when immutable truths were first starting to be supplanted by whatever the next great Chicxulub impactor asteroid known as Facebook declared them to be. I was completely oblivious to the reality that by making this grand journey, I had created no end of heartache for Megan and Alena, and had driven away the only woman who ever really loved me—who didn't also have it as her express intention to murder me in my sleep.

As I jumped out of bed on Monday, November 2, 2009, I did what I always do in these sticky situations. I quickly compartmentalized all that I had reflected upon the day before. I immediately buried it all deep in some sullen recess at the back corner of my brain. It was a trick I'd learned when I was very little. When you're too tiny to fight, and the thought of being sodomized at some reform school in Guelph precludes any suggestion of flight, you find a way to operationalize your primordial instincts to survive by getting your brain to do it for you. As the master of constructed reality, it didn't take me long to focus instead on just how God damn amazing I was—and how impervious I'd be to ever having to face the kind of earthshattering calamity coming my way in just four short days. So pathetically childish, right?

So here I was, living as a single parent with Megan and Alena at the most prestigious address in downtown Vancouver: the much talked about Venus tower situated at 1239 West Georgia. We were on the 23$^{rd}$ floor, and had the most amazing view of the ocean and the North Shore Mountains. It was like living at 5$^{th}$ Avenue and East 59$^{th}$ in Manhattan, near Central Park. It was the kind of neighbourhood where you could go out for a nice walk and randomly run into the likes of Kim Cattrall, Bif Naked and Virginia Madsen. Six months earlier, Elton John and Elvis Costello asked if they could pet my dog Lupin as they walked elbow-to-elbow down Bute Street toward the seawall at Coal Harbour. Our upstairs neighbour Brandy was still reeling from that fracas stirred up by Ben Affleck and one of her exotic dancer employees back in 2003 at her internationally famous strip club, but all and all, things were good. The global economy had tanked the previous year, but we, as a loving family, were doing well. Megan had graduated from high school in 2008 and was working at a trendy clothing store up on Robson. Alena was in Grade 12 at King George Secondary, just two blocks from that stunning grove of palm trees over near English Bay. She was getting straight A's, and was quite active in sports. She was now well on her way to achieving her childhood dream of getting into UBC and setting herself up to become a veterinarian. To say both daughters were being spoiled terribly by their father at this time would be an understatement in the extreme. I constantly lavished them with the very best in teen amenities. Well aware of their pampered Coal Harbour lifestyle, they often joked that they were the Grabbdashians. For her milestone 19$^{th}$ birthday five months earlier, I took Megan shopping on Rodeo Drive down in Los Angeles. For her sweet 16 birthday nearly one year ago, I took Alena to Manhattan for a Broadway show and a weekend of fine dining on Park Avenue. That leisurely Sunday afternoon we spent up at the Bronx Zoo with waffle cones was the best part of the whole deal. Having re-partnered, Marianne was sadly living 2200 miles away in Ottawa. It would be years before we'd learn of her most unbearable anguish. It would be even longer before I'd realize that spending $16,000 to send Lupin away to summer camp to play frisbee golf and get her nails done on Texada Island was probably not such a good idea.

As I jumped into the shower that morning, to get ready for my Helijet flight to Victoria for some client meetings, I reflected once again on how I got to this unusual place of success. It came down to the fact that back when I was overseeing that information technology project, tangentially connected to the Scarborough rapist case, I had apparently made such a lasting impression on the IT vendor community that many of them tried to headhunt me to come work for them. Some cited my public executive program certificate from the School of Business at Queen's University as one of the reasons for their strong interest. It took them two years to get my attention, but I finally relented. I left the RCMP as a superintendent on a Friday afternoon in 2006. By Monday morning I was already working as a fat-salary executive consultant at the fifth largest IT company in the world: a Montreal-based multinational, then known as CGI Management Consulting and Information Systems Inc. I spent the next 12 months travelling across Canada, learning the ropes and being billed out at market rates to multiple public sector organizations. I sponged up everything there was to know about executive leadership, people and culture enrichment, business process improvement, marketing and communications, and digital-tech investment planning. When all the national travel got too much for a responsible single parent to handle, I decided to leave CGI in order to start my own consulting company back home in Vancouver.

All my friends said that launching my own firm in the middle of an economic downturn was a longshot—akin to me going from Walmart greeter to astronaut. But with a little bit of luck, and lots of hard work, it ended up working out just fine. Somehow I pulled it off. It was pretty much what Mr. McConnell said would happen one day. To celebrate my first million, I quietly went out and bought myself a gold Rolex watch. Soon came my purchase of that slick Porsche 928 that I'd seen Tom Cruise ditch into Lake Michigan in the film, *Risky Business*. This afternoon Helijet would be whisking me away across the Salish Sea so I could continue on with my latest contract: helping to guide a proposed $49 million investment in IT at a high-profile Crown corporation. If only Carole Taylor were still Minister of Finance. I used to have such a total schoolyard crush on her back when she used to sit near me in that always crowded, always conversation-quiet aircraft. It's too bad she left high office for new beginnings in 2008. As a girl-shy teenager from Scarborough it was a big deal for me to be commuting to the office every week in a commercial jet helicopter—and to have Miss Toronto 1964 sit so close. To pass the time on our short ocean skimming flights I would often imagine she was Agent 99 and I was a more debonaire version of Maxwell Smart, both secretly working together to counter the forces of human stupidity. In my mind of course this meant taking on the likes of IBM, Deloitte and KPMG and all the many assistant deputy ministers who incessantly engage them to help government become more proficient at failing sooner, and at a far better price point. It was a thread of quixotic fantasy and self-deception that made me feel like big man on campus. I only wish I had had the courage to go over and say hi to her. Missed it by that much, I guess.

So when I rolled out of bed the very next day—on Tuesday, November 3, 2009—I was immediately thrust into this curious state of primordial worry. Yesterday's meeting with the CIO at that Crown corporation had gone very well—and he couldn't have been any more pleased with how things were progressing. But overnight, and again this morning on the local television news, there had been a number of disconcerting reports about the global swine-flu pandemic that was currently sweeping the planet. It was being said that the elderly and young people with robust immune response systems were at particular risk for hospitalization, or worse, sudden death. Over the past two weeks around 52 teenagers had died from H1N1 across Canada. Grieving parents were on the television news every evening—crying to high heaven about their inconceivable losses. Yet, the vaccine rollout in B.C. was still focused on toddlers, seniors and primary school kids. Megan and Alena weren't in line to get their vaccination shots for at least two more weeks. I was scared shitless. As someone who once worked on shaping pandemic response policies for police officers in a first responder setting, I fully understood what a failure to act quickly on the part of humanity would mean for so many unsuspecting families. My last road trip as an RCMP officer was when I attended a U.S. Homeland Security conference in Washington, D.C. on emergency response planning, back in the spring of 2006. His name escapes me now, but some Italian American infectious disease expert with a cheeky Brooklyn accent—and a contagious dry sense of humour—warned us that if we as a species didn't heed all the harsh lessons of the Spanish flu pandemic of 1918 we'd all one day witness untold misery all across North America. He forewarned that the third wave is always the most deadly. He even went so far as to confidently say that our more modern and thus more self-engrossed world could be susceptible to a completely unheard of fourth wave. I found it hard to believe the human race could ever be so stupid to let that happen, but I took his word for it. After all, he was the accredited scientist, and I was just some non-medically trained layperson with zero grounding in epidemiology. I knew it was best for me to just stick to my knitting.

As Alena headed out the door for school on the morning of Wednesday, November 4, 2009, I took note of the fact she looked a little pale and wasn't quite herself. Being the overly paranoid helicopter parent that I was, I placed my hand on her forehead to see if she had a fever. It was just fine, but I couldn't help launching into one of my trademark soliloquies about the meaning of the universe, and the perils of impending doom. I was trying to tell Alena about H1N1, asking that she keep me posted on her how she was feeling. Tired of hearing me ramble all the time, Alena swung her backpack over her shoulder, stomped her feet into her Uggs, and said, "What ev's, dad." She probably never forgave me for that rather embarrassing time when I attempted to tie back her ponytail using a plastic zap strap from Home Depot. And when it came to picking out stylin' skirts and tops from Aritzia—and buying feminine hygiene products over at London Drugs—I was as useless as a grandparent at a Justin Bieber concert.

As Megan stumbled out of bed mid-morning that day, I tried to no avail to also warn her about what was going on with this global swine-flu pandemic. She said her teen friend Tina Lovgreen had told her all about it, so she wasn't really worried. She reminded me Tina was an aspiring photo-journalist who might one day become a famous reporter. I couldn't argue with that logic, after all it was Tina who got Megan into Richard's on Richards underage so the two of them could chill backstage with some emerging pop star by the name of Lady Gaga. Hey, this was the kind of proud father anecdote that always reminded me of that moment when the obstetrician first handed Megan to me in the maternity ward back in May of 1990. As Sinéad O'Connor belted out *Nothing Compares 2 U* in the background, I looked into her peepers and said, "Daddy will always protect you." What I saw in those eyes was fire, determination, and a mischievous glance that seemed to be saying, "I'll take it from here, Dad." What I saw when I said the exact same thing to baby Alena in November of 1992 was high intelligence, profound introspection, and a worrisome gaze that was clearly communicating, "Oh fuck, this can't be good."

So off into the world my two precious angels went that fateful day: one to Grade 12 as the recently elected co-president of her student council, the other to her store to peddle pricy jeans and gangster hoodies to luminaries and hapless Point Grey students. But by supper time both were back home in bed, writhing in absolute flu agony. Both had very high fevers. Both were suffering from severe sore throats and God-awful joint pains. Both were crying out for their mom. It was shaping up to be my very worst nightmare. So off I went like a chicken with his bloody head cut off, putting on that silly June Cleaver apron, scrambling to rustle up soup and a shitload of Tylenol. Again, it was all to no avail. They just got sicker and sicker. And by bedtime Alena was vomiting non-stop.

If only Marianne were here. She'd know what to do. She really would. I was lost. I was out of my element. On the wall in my den was a commendation that I'd received in 1998 from the Director of the FBI for helping to launch a joint FBI-RCMP task force that brought down a prominent organized crime group based out of Boston—and thwarted a contract killing slated to happen up in Vancouver across the street from Science World. Over on the fireplace mantle was an empty bottle of Dom that I'd kept as a memento for hunting down—and extraditing back to Canada from Manila—a senior court official charged with molesting six children back in B.C. On the minimalist design coffee table in our living room was a copy of the book *Abuse of Trust* by Christopher Hyde. It was a nonfiction piece that chronicled my lead detective role in the 1989 arrest of Dr. James Stewart Tyhurst: the former Allan Memorial Institute intern and department head emeritus from the UBC department of psychiatry who'd raped countless female patients over several decades using the very

CIA brainwashing techniques he helped to perfect in the 1950s under Project MKUltra. What the book didn't mention was my courageous decision to execute a search warrant on the office of the College of Physicians and Surgeons of British Columbia in order to unearth the dirty little secret that prior allegations against this quack doctor had gone unreported. His actions had simply been rationalized by the Canadian medical profession as questionable science that was worthy of peer group admonishment and clinical reconsideration, but not swift intervention by competent law enforcement authorities like me who actually investigated serial rape for a living.

Perplexingly—despite all my experience and acclaim dealing with immense danger and dark complexity—I just froze in my tracks. It was so incredibly frustrating. I could be trusted to participate in the ransom drop in 1990 when Jimmy Pattison's daughter was kidnapped by a gang of meth heads. I could program manage this $49 million Crown investment in modern IT. Nobody even blinked an eye when I threw-in on the close quarter protection of Queen Elizabeth and the Duke of Edinburgh when they were in town for the Commonwealth Heads of Government Meeting in 1987—as they made their way through a boisterous crowd at the Vancouver art gallery, across the street from their suite at the Four Seasons. My gold embossed invite to personally meet the Queen in person still adorns the china cabinet in my dining room. For Heaven's sake, I could even go on national television on short notice and speak credibly to the intricacies of Air India, APEC and Bingogate. As far as I was aware, I was the only Mountie ever interviewed for an episode of ABC's 20-20. Yet on this particular night—the very night that a deadly global pandemic was ravaging families all across Canada—I had no clue what to do to protect my very own daughters. What if they really did have H1N1? Where would I take them? What medicine could they get? Which hospital might take them in? How would we even get there? All the radio stations were saying if you have the swine flu just stay home and ride it out, don't come to the ER and infect everyone else. It was all I could do that evening to not curl up in a fetal position and cry. I was so mad at myself. I just couldn't figure out why I was acting like such a child. Where was this all coming from? I was in my own house, but I just wanted to go home. I had no end of luxury at my feet, but I just wanted to go climb an apple tree and play on the monkey bars with my stupid brothers. Something inside of me was screaming to come out. I had no idea it would take the most frightening moment of my entire life to finally find out what it was. I had no idea what lay in store for me just around the corner.

**CHAPTER 3:** Where Poetry is Written

WHEN I GOT OUT OF BED on the morning of Thursday, November 5, 2009, I swore I would do better. Much better. I really would. I was sorry and I didn't mean to be bad. I'd be a good boy now. I knew just what to do. I reverted to the kind of behaviour that very often—but not always—kept my tormentor at bay, back when I was very little. I did my chores. I walked the dog. I scrubbed the toilets. I put away the laundry and organized my socks and underpants with drill-sergeant precision. I took out the trash. Heck, I even helped old lady MacPherson load boxes into her Oldsmobile down in the parkade. Most critically, I arranged all the designer furniture, fashion magazines and knickknacks around our apartment in such a manner so as to achieve perfect visual alignment and complete aesthetic symmetry. Alena would always ride my ass for being such an insufferable OCD freak. She was particularly bewildered by my silly habit of incessantly bending over and picking up dark, asymmetrical pieces of lint from our creamy white wall-to-wall carpets. What she couldn't possibly know is that for a person like me—with my embattled childhood—if I were to lose my ability to control the universe, and everything in it, it would soon start to control me. I'd soon be in a world of appalling hurt.

When I checked in on the girls I noticed Megan was feeling a bit better, but Alena was taking a giant turn for the worse. I connected with Marianne on the telephone and was given nurturing mother instructions on how to best administer suppository Gravol. For that task, I called upon Megan to do the nasty part. I mentioned to Marianne that they were saying on the radio this morning that some Asian woman with asthma had just died from the swine flu last Sunday after Richmond General Hospital sent her home twice—telling her to stay away from the ER. I said it was going to be an uphill battle getting any hospital to take us in. She wasted no time saying, "If it comes down to it, Russ, just get them to the ER right away, and don't take any guff off those fuck stick nurses."

Hearing Marianne loud and clear, I quickly got the girls over to see Dr. Mazzarella at the Seymour Health Centre up on 7th Avenue. It was just a short family doctor consultation. It was bad. Although blood tests would still have to be taken to be sure, he confirmed the worst: both were said to have presumptive H1N1. Both were issued prescriptions for Tamiflu and ordered to immediately quarantine at home—and to remain bedridden until further notice. Compartmentalizing my simmering fear, I instantly clicked into Jason Bourne mode. When I worked as a first-responder constable in Richmond in the mid-1980s, I personally observed that the ER staff there tended to be nothing more than a bunch of doubting-Thomas oddballs. Richmond General was out. When I worked as a homicide detective back in the late 1980s, early 1990s, I noticed that Vancouver General had pretty good staff, but they were often too busy dealing with too many routine walk-ins to properly recognize an ID, or infectious disease emergency. So they were out. Lions Gate Hospital over on the north shore was pretty decent, but they were too far away. Then I remembered that when I did a 6-month rotational stint on the drug squad at North Vancouver Detachment in 1979 they sent me off to train for two weeks with some narcs from VPD's street crew in the Downtown Eastside. It was when I grew a beard and had long hair, and walked around doing drug busts looking just like Al Pacino in *Serpico*. Through that eye-opening experience I learned that the only ER that seemed equipped to deal with differential response emergencies, and to spot a walking-dead ID patient coming through the door, was St. Paul's Hospital up on Burrard. Here in 2009, the Downtown Eastside—which is primarily serviced by St. Paul's—is said to have the highest per capita rate of HIV-AIDS infections related to chronic IV drug use anywhere in the world outside of Africa. By all official government and academic accounts it is also said to be the most destitute, and frankly, most forgotten urban neighbourhood in all of Canada. The level of human suffering that exists there is unequalled anywhere in North America. We sanctimonious Canadians simply step right over it on our way downtown to buy pricy jeans and gangster hoodies. So I knew what I had to do. If either of the girls needed to go to the ER, there would be no call to 9-1-1. No ambulance crew telling me what for. No bossy business associate from my company telling me to grow up and simply follow standard protocol. If it ever came down to that moment, I would carry them both on my back to St. Paul's Hospital. There would be no stopping me. No stopping me at all.

The very next day—on Friday, November 6, 2009—I got up with brisk urgency at 4:00 a.m., and once again checked in on poor Alena. She was burning up with a high fever. She was vomiting uncontrollably. She was delirious and talking gibberish. At 6:00 a.m. she staggered out of her bedroom and collapsed into a shivering ball on the cold and unwelcoming Spanish tile floor out in our cavernous front foyer. I was no doctor, but I had been to enough scenes of death, and had audited over 20 autopsies. I recognized that penetrating look on Alena's face. It was that familiar look of vacant hope that sends shutters down the spine of even the most heartless prick. I knew this could be it, so I called out to Megan to ask her to come help me get Alena ready for the short trip over to St. Paul's—and to confirm if she'd be okay with staying home alone without me, for who knows how long. Sick as a dog, Megan said she'd be fine, that she'd keep me posted. She placed both hands on my cheeks, stared deep into my eyes like an adoring parent, and said, "Stay calm, Dad. I believe in you. You can do this." Within minutes, I was carrying Alena into a taxi downstairs with instructions to the driver to step on it. He took one look at us and knew just what he had to do. Being a benevolent Sikh immigrant, he got us there quick and waived his much needed fare without any hesitation.

As I burst through the doors of the ER at St. Paul's with Alena in my arms, I yelled out to the triage nurse standing at the main entrance, "H1N1!" It was all I needed to say. Within seconds two additional nurses were leaping over the counter, helping me position Alena into an empty wheelchair. Her face was beet red, and she was slumped over sideways. As I shuffled toward the admitting clerk, to take care of the paperwork, what appeared to be a stoic charge nurse yelled out from behind the counter, "Get her to acute care, stat." The male nurse who was attending to Alena thirty feet away replied, "I'm just getting her vitals for the chart." To the jaw-drop amazement of the 26 homeless people cobbled together in the waiting room, the charge nurse yelled back, "I can fucking tell what her vitals are, just by looking at her. Get her to acute care now, negative pressure room, stretcher 10, and alert ICU."

My instincts had been correct. Alena would be well cared for now. Only St. Paul's could possibly know what to do. Only they could recognize a downward-spiral ID patient at 50 paces. It wasn't that they possessed some sort of modern-medicine crystal ball. It wasn't as if only the very best practitioners in town worked there. And judging by the shabby 1950s curb appeal of the joint, it certainly wasn't because they benefitted from the best in facilities and equipment. It was because they—by no intentional design of their own—were obliged to work on the very frontlines of the absolutely unspeakable. By necessity, they were required every day to confront Canada's most shameful secret. I'm talking about that ragged 30-square block area of wretched loneliness and abandoned agony called the Downtown Eastside—a forlorn urban community of broken souls discarded by the callous and the indifferent right in the very center of what all the Scandinavian experts assert is the most livable and opulent city in the world. What better place to host the 2010 Winter Olympics, right? Only 12 short weeks away now. By necessity the medical staff here are always ready, willing and able to welcome the sickest of all sick, free of any personal-preservation hesitance, socio-economic bias, or microaggression judgement. If you ask me, the homeless and the addicted congregate at St. Paul's, not because they have the sniffles or a twisted ankle, but because it's the only place where they feel valued, safe, and appreciated. I saw the same thing 30 years ago in 1979. It was back when I was that 22-year-old wretch searching for some place to unleash—and let fucking fly—my own healthy measure of simmering rage and unbearable rejection.

I was no philosopher, no genius, but it struck me this morning that this might just be the kind of setting where—if I wasn't careful—I too might be thrust into the warm waiting arms of long-evaded redemption. I'd probably not even see it coming. The pain of having to confront all that shame would be beyond the pale. I had a bad feeling about all this. I would have to watch my step today or else 52 tightly choreographed years of convincing myself she couldn't possibly have done all those vile things to me might unravel faster than you could ever say: "Russell, get over here! I'm just sick of hearing all the ladies down at Steinberg's going on and on about how handsome you are, while we're trying to get the God damn groceries done for Heaven's sake. And what about my smart new outfit? What was the point of me even putting it on? Your father has gone back out to have a closer look at that fancy new Chatelaine house up in Bramalea's H-section, but he'll be back within the hour. Your brothers and sisters are out in the yard, or with their friends or something. So get on your knees, right this very minute, and show mommy how sorry you are. How dare you embarrass your mother like that? Who do you think you are? You're just seven years old, and only in Grade 2 for Christ's sake. Now lick harder. Harder I said. Harder like I told you a hundred times before, you disgusting barnyard animal excuse for a human being! Honestly, just go to your room. I'm done with you."

So while I might—this very second—be standing in the emergency medicine entrance of some incorruptible inner city hospital, I was also undeniably now on the veritable doorstep of something imminently catastrophic. This could very well be the end of my beginning. If I could only hang in there just a little bit longer, maybe some previously overlooked thread of evidence will emerge from the great void that will prove it was all made up in my head the whole bloody time. Now that would be one neat and tidy way of making it all go away, wouldn't it? No ill-gotten delusion there. No setting myself up for some calamitous plunge into the great abyss as George Orwell once foresaw in his divinatory reflections on where poetry is really written. Just some long overlooked cold case from the long-forgotten 1960s silently put to rest, right?

# CHAPTER 4: A Child's Last Moments

THERE HAD BEEN such a whirlwind of activity today that frankly I was having a hard time keeping it all straight. I wasn't even sure who I really was any more. It was almost as if I was on my way to becoming a completely different person than that guy who just last Sunday was wallowing in all his Coal Harbour glory. My watch said it was 4:06 p.m., but that just didn't seem to make any sense. I remember now that it all began with our thunderous arrival at triage intake around 7:30 a.m. As Alena was swept away in that wobbly wheelchair—slumped over like a winded ragdoll—I finished up with the admitting clerk who signed off on her data entry by tapping me gently on the back of the hand, saying, "Man, I wouldn't want to be in your shoes. She's going to be okay, I'm pretty sure of it. Just follow the orange arrows on the floor, and head on over to acute care. She's in good hands now." Since this was essentially a Catholic nursing hospital by origin—founded by the Sisters of Providence back in 1894 as a gesture to blunt the surge of disease and injury arising from the Klondike gold rush of the 1890s—I wasn't sure if by good hands she meant brilliant practitioners experienced with treating critically ill teenagers, or that fucking prick up in Heaven who stood by and did absolutely nothing while that deranged swine had her fucking way with a shy little monkey who just wanted to finish his chores and go play baseball with all the other kids over at the park. Alena was just nine days away from her 17th birthday—and the most adorable little peanut you could ever hope to lay your eyes on—so I was expecting much more from everyone today. The very life of my second born child was on the line here. I just knew that if God forbid she were to suddenly up and die, before she even had a chance to graduate from high school, there would be no way anyone could stop me from joining her in Heaven. My entire thread of personal survival on this godforsaken planet was wrapped up in raising those two pigtail-pretty girls in an anguish-free encasement of quixotic escapism— within which the two of them would never have to go through what I endured as an innocent child. From the very day my own mother attempted to murder me in 1965 in that shallow sink of bathroom tap water, feathering and preening this elaborate nest of protective delusion was all that I ever knew. To let it slip away now would mean having to confront all the trauma of pleading for my life, discharging my bowels in my underpants, and nearly dying from watery suffocation at age 8. It would mean finally having to accept that the prepositioned and unzipped hockey equipment bag on that bathroom floor wasn't really there to take used towels over to the Goodwill box. It would mean I would no longer have any safe place to run and hide. I would have no patience today for the clinical reconsideration of human stupidity—or the stone-hearted indifference of blind-eye Deities.

As I stood up and turned around to make my way on over to acute care, I was instantly struck by the collective sentiment of good will being directed my way by all the homeless and addicted folk assembled together in the waiting room. From a distance, with squinty eyes, the place kinda resembled that rabble-laden cantina in the *Star Wars* movie I remembered seeing at Capital Six in the fall of 1977—when I was 20 years old. Suffering from disease and injury no mainstream Canadian could ever contemplate, this tiny wretched hive of scum and villainy somehow found the decency to throw me an affectionate smile of reassurance. Some tipped their tattered Vancouver Canucks ballcaps. Others stood and placed their right hand over their heart as if they were in the presence of some great war hero. One horribly emaciated young man who never once looked up from his chair called out with a raspy old-geezer voice and said, "Feel for you, brother." As I rounded the corner to begin my long walk of parental trepidation, an Indigenous woman in her late sixties stopped me cold and handed me a noticeably rancid turkey sandwich from 7-11. She said she found it discarded in some Smithrite over on Pender and Gore. She said the Creator had told her just now that I was going to be here for a while. She wanted me to have her last meal because she knew I wouldn't have time to grab something on my own later on in the day. It was all I could do to keep it together as I walked down that brightly lit hallway. What the fuck? Such incredible kindness from such warm-hearted people. Maybe there was at least one benevolent God up in Heaven after all. Maybe I just hadn't been properly introduced. Not yet, anyway. Maybe it was time for me to start looking into what all the Indigenous peoples seem to know about meaning and purpose that we colonial imperialist fucks don't. I always thought Marianne might be some sort of divine angel sent from above to rescue me, but now, thanks to my irascible childhood trait of never standing still—and always being on the run from anything that even remotely smacked of maternal grace—she was gone and I'd probably never get her back.

As I entered the acute care area of the emergency department I saw what appeared to be a dozen or so beds occupied by some very sick people—six on one side, six on the other. Nurses and doctors in full protective garb were rushing from station to station, doing lots of busy stuff in rapid succession. Over on the left side—halfway down the open air ward—I could see Alena lying on her back on a gurney inside a glass-enclosed room that kinda looked like a giant fishbowl. I guess that's what they meant by a negative pressure room; something that would most likely keep her suspected H1N1 infection from spreading to other patients until they could be certain she was no longer contagious. As I approached I felt really good that things finally seemed to be under such sensible control. Alena was now where she needed to be and would likely be home for supper later on tonight after a precautionary infusion of saline solution and a routine dose of hospital-grade acetaminophen. Megan had just called me on my flip phone to say she was doing just fine—and as always, still very much in charge of being in charge back at the ranch. Marianne had packed a suitcase, and was on standby to fly out from Ottawa, if on the very off chance things did in fact go south. My Crown corporation client over in Victoria—whose wife was a primary care physician—had emailed me earlier in the morning to say, "Good luck, I'm sure everything will be fine. Take your time, and don't be in any hurry to get back to the project. Family comes first, you know." My word, what a relief. Everything seemed to be coming together so nicely. Well, just as tickety-boo organized as anyone could ever reasonably expect them to be—especially for a plucky little OCD worrywart like me.

As I got closer to Alena I felt the usual degree of mild concern that of course any normal parent might feel whenever one of their precious little munchkins is forced to fend off some sort of random, pain-in-the-arse infection. As I entered her glass room with a skip in my step and boundless hope in my heart I instantly froze. I totally lost my shit. It was all I could do to not scream at the top of my lungs. This wasn't good. Not good at all. From the patient monitor located just above her head I could see that Alena's heart was racing out of control. Her blood pressure was quite low, and her body temperature was soaring. In addition to having shallow respiration, her oxygen sats were dipping well into the low 90s. Most alarmingly, Alena had a bloated and eggplant-purple face that made her look like that pulverized Alex Jones character from the film *Prisoners*, after he'd been repeatedly punched in the face by Hugh Jackman. She didn't say much because she kept gasping for air, but through the tiny slits in her barely opened puffy eyes I could see that her salty tears were trying to say, "Oh my God, Dad. I've never before felt this sick. It's unbearable. I just wish mommy were here. Mommy, please, where are you?"

That was the moment when everything in the broader celestial universe changed—and I do mean everything. That was when all the searing fear started to mount: slowly at first, but then with increasing Sabretooth intensity as the day progressed. Yes, human history was about to record that this would be the exact geographic location on planet Earth where—despite all my best efforts as a father to always protect my children—there would be an incomprehensible death in the family tonight. At the young age of 16, our precious little Alena was slipping away. She was being ravaged by insufferable torment. It was unstoppable and there was nothing I could do about it. Strangely enough, all the sounds of her desperate gurgling and gasping for breath triggered an intense pounding memory in my brain of colouring books and Crayola crayons. The alluring scent of all that pigmented wax with such bright pastel iridescence was both comforting and terrifying at the same time. Maybe it was because, as a young child, Alena had always been so good at colouring pretty pictures of the Easter Bunny and little Maggie Simpson. Maybe it was because in the moments leading up to my gruesome drowning in 1965 I had been sitting on the living room floor of that despicable family home on Brentwood Drive in Bramalea—colouring up a storm with all my Johnny Quest colouring books—when I was lured into the upstairs bathroom on the pretext and promise of a receiving a special treat from that sex offender who loved me just as passionately as she hated me. Falling for that trick not only ravaged me with the sudden terrorizing jolt of imminent death, it encased me in layers of shame and despair that far outweighed any of the agony I felt when I finally succumbed to the grotesque inhalation of all that stinging-nostril sink water—and fell despondently soiled and unconscious on that bathroom floor. Were it not for that oblivious older sister who happened by—and wondered what all the commotion might be—there's no doubt in my mind I would have ended up dead and discarded in that hockey bag. My last pleasant sensation as a living, breathing human being would have been the warm and soothing scent of Crayola crayons.

So here I was—again at 4:06 p.m.—sitting on this motherfucking prick plastic chair just outside the trauma room, wondering what the hell was going to happen next. After first seeing Alena in such a desperate state earlier today, I of course immediately got on the blower and told Marianne to head to the Ottawa airport right away, and get on the very next flight to Vancouver. She said she would move heaven and earth to do so, but it would be a tall order because WestJet had just grounded all flights worldwide due to a complete collapse of their global reservation system—and because Air Canada was having such a hard time keeping up with all the spillover demand. As the day progressed with such soul-crushing misery I had multiple sidebar huddles with a small army of clinicians who kept telling me they would do everything they could. They even showed me Alena's chest film, stressing with great unease that she had full bilateral whiteout of the lungs. It was medical speak for unsurvivable virial pneumonia. Her lungs were slowly filling with suffocating fluids and her oxygenation was on the verge of total collapse. She was drowning right before our very eyes. Yes drowning, and all these specialists were now of the shared belief that this might be far more than H1N1. Subject to further bloodwork and lab cultures, their working diagnosis was that this was most likely an advanced-progression case of streptococcal toxic shock syndrome—something that almost always kills teenaged girls within a matter of hours. It was surging through all her vital organs unabated, and the purple discoloration and bloating that I'd seen earlier had now spread to her entire body. Her precious baby-girl skin was so tightly stretched, and her face was so puffy with agony, it actually looked like she might explode any minute. It was unbearable to watch.

So in the midst of all this rising action drama and grand befuddlement, I was somehow supposed to be grateful that Alena had just been moved over to the trauma room where she would be given high-dose infusions of therapeutics and broad-spectrum antimicrobials. From my prior time as a first-responder cop I of course knew that the trauma room was essentially the front lobby of the hospital morgue. What kept me somewhat hopeful was being told that the ICU had just sent a four-person critical care team downstairs to take over full conduct of her chart. I guess I was also expected to be over-the-moon delighted that the hospital had just assigned Alena her very own personal social worker. She was an indelibly pleasant woman who reminded me of Jean Byron, the actress who played Patty Duke's mom on television in 1963. She followed me everywhere I went, and even stood outside in the hallway when I went to the bathroom. Then suddenly, just like that sinister Stephen Baldwin scene from the movie *The Usual Suspects*: strangest thing. Yup, strangest thing. Around 2:00 p.m. this social worker leaned over to me with a deadpan stare and said, "You know Russell, these healthy teenagers, these stubborn little buggers, you know they fight, and they fight, but eventually their little hearts give out. If you want, I can get you a pencil and a notepad. You can start a journal. I think it might just help you cope." A pencil and a fucking notepad, are you fucking kidding me! What in God's name did either of these two things have to do with anything? I'm sure she was just trying to be helpful, but come on, give me a fucking break. Honestly, you'd swear I was the God damn patient over here. Despite everything Alena was going through, she was treating me as if I was the one who was in crisis and about to die. As always—with the mind and maturity of a nearly murdered 8 year old—I was completely oblivious to what was really going on here.

As the supper hour approached, the head of the ICU, Dr. Gregory Grant, took me aside and asked me straight up, "Do you and your ex-wife get along?" I replied, "Yes of course, why?" He replied back with a calm Ward Cleaver voice, "We've reached a critical moment here, Russ. I suggest she come as quickly as possible." After telling him that I had just found out moments ago that Marianne had finally been able to secure a standby seat on an inbound Air Canada flight from Toronto, he swung his fatherly arm over my shoulders and said, "We're going to do everything we can, you know that, right? We'll try a central IV. We'll escalate to transfusion and plasma if we have to. Worst case scenario, we'll place Alena in an induced coma. She'll be on a ventilator. It won't be pretty, but it'll stabilize her oxygen sats. It'll help her reach burst suppression. Right now her brain is under such great strain. It's cooking like a fried egg. But we have to brace ourselves here, Russ. We have to be ready for that less than happy outcome. If you look over at the patient monitor, you'll see that Alena's heart rate is 172. It's been that way since early morning. If you add up the hours involved, it means she has run three back-to-back Boston marathons in a row, and is still going. Even worse, her oxygen sats are falling below 80 percent and her fever has just spiked at 104.5. With a blood pressure of just 58 over 20, she really hasn't got much time left. These are what we call vitals incompatible with life."

Having long compartmentalized all discernible reality, I of course responded by saying, "I get it. I understand. I trust your judgement. We'll do what we have to do. I'm sure it'll all be fine. But doc, come on, I gotta ask. Why in God's name has Alena been assigned a damn social worker? She's been following me around all day. We both know Alena doesn't need a bloody social worker. We both know she actually needs a medical miracle for Heaven sake. I just don't get it."

I had seen a lot of pain and suffering in my time. I had experienced no end of shock and terror in my youth. No question my 1965 drowning was a big one. I'm loath to say much more about all those acts of forced sex in my early childhood, but being held upside down by my ankles over that high-floor balcony at 3:10 a.m. at the Holiday Inn in Windsor when I was 9 was certainly a doozy too. Had my mother let go I would have ended up swimming for my life in the icy waters of the Detroit River below. To this day, I still have an uncontrollable phobia of high heights and green coloured river water. To this day, I still wake up at 3:10 a.m. to scan the room for the sound of approaching whatever. For over five decades I almost always placed a spare set of runners beside my bed—just in case I had to make a run for it. Being chained half naked to a backyard fence in Etobicoke in the dead of winter at age 3 was also one for the ages, that's for sure. Having to explain to daddy why the hell I had God damn frostbite on my cheeks when he came home from work was actually the scariest part of the whole terrifying ordeal. As far as constant childhood beatings go, I wouldn't even know where to begin. I would reach the commendable age of 57 before an eminent plastic surgeon would be ready to harvest a rib from my right torso to rebuild a nose so unthinkably pulverized by so many juvenile fractures. On the RCMP side of things, those two innocent little girls being burnt alive in that housefire in Lions Bay in December of 1977 still stands out as the most grisly thing I ever had to deal with while on duty. Being tricked by those two homicide investigators into serving as the exhibit custodian at their double autopsy at Lions Gate Hospital was an act of cruelty in and of itself. I was just 20 years old and the grotesque sight and penetrating smell of all that charred baby-girl skin falling off those tiny bones was something that haunted me for years. The searing heat from that housefire had been so intense that the pink flannel fabric of those adorable little PJs had melted right into their tender flesh. The pathologist told me both girls were still very much alive when this happened. They weren't afforded the mercy of death by smoke inhalation. They both suffered immeasurably. Learning that their very own mom would soon be held negligent for causing the fire prompted me to flat out stop eating. Convinced there was no God, believing all mothers were killers, I pulled a Karen Carpenter. I lost 40 lbs. and was admitted just seven weeks later to the very same hospital with myocarditis and a raging case of anorexia scurvy. It would be 30 years before I could once again stand the smell of barbequed chicken. It would be six months before all my head hair finally grew back, after falling off in smelly tangled clumps on the bathroom floor. The dark hair that fell off my forearms that week never did grow back. To this very day, I still have creepy white forearms with not a single manly human hair in sight.

And while I'm heading down this rabbit hole of lived experience I may as well mention that dropping by BC Children's Hospital in May of 1993 in order to get non-accidental trauma details from Dr. Hlady, and observe a 2-year-old girl lying completely naked, comatose, and heartbreakingly alone on a small gurney in the pediatric ICU—with hideous tubes coming out of her trachea and vagina—really didn't sit well with me either. It was just two days after her very own mother had grabbed her by the ankles and centrifugally swung her tiny infant skull directly into a sharp-edged coffee table back at the family home in Boston Bar. It was not unlike being called out to the scene of that fatal hit and run in Chilliwack in August of 1991. I was an off-duty homicide detective at the time, but the local collision analyst was having a hard time piecing it all together because the decapitated pedestrian lying in middle of the road was the teenaged son of an RCMP officer back at the office. Anxious to get back home to Marianne and 2-year-old Megan, I wasted no time in arresting our prime eyewitness at the scene. Apparently I was the only cop there who noticed the guy still had oozing brain matter on his front bumper. It has never been lost on me that all but one of these unthinkable tales of suffering and sorrow involve a heartless psychotic mother—and a cowed father who almost always turns a blind eye.

As you might have surmised, none of this exposure to some of the most horrific sights and smells that any sane human could ever imagine having to endure could ever prepare me for what Dr. Grant was about to say in response to my bold question about that social worker. After careful measured reflection, he looked at me very directly and said, "She's not a social worker, Russ. She's a grief counselor, and she's not here for Alena, she's here for you." It was his way of telling me Alena would soon be dead. It was the universe's way of telling me there would be no more wallowing in Coal Harbour glory. No more playing the wounded child card in order to avoid having to face the realities of how it really was on this earth. No more deluding myself that all my remarkable success in the RCMP—and now here in business consulting—was just some adorable accident. I was now so rattled with gripping Sabretooth tiger fear that there was frankly no room left for anything else in my soul in any event. I could barely catch my breath, and just like in all the movies there was both a loud ringing sound in my ears and the sense that everything around me was moving in 'go ask Alice' slow motion. What would happen next in that trauma room would turn out to be the very thing that every loving parent fears the most. Right before my eyes, Alena would have a scalpel slice an incision in her bare chest while she was still very much conscious and burning up with torturous fever. It was so a Costco-sized catheter could be carefully threaded into her heart to get her Hail Mary plasma transfusion underway. Right before my eyes, Alena would squeal like a horrifically wounded rabbit trapped in the jaws of a vicious predator. Right before my eyes, all the interns and nurses present were themselves tearing up. Between the pain of that heavy-gauge metal guide wire being shoved directly into her subclavian vein—and the burning heat of that rubber surgical drape being flopped across her face—it was all she could do to stay conscious. It was all she could do to catch her breath. I was so scared I was quite certain I was going to have a heart attack right on the spot. I distinctly remember thinking to myself, "This cannot be happening. I didn't come all this way. I didn't go through so much torment and torture, and overcome so much heartache and sorrow, and live long enough to help shepherd two beautiful daughters through to adulthood—free of savage evisceration—just to see it all it taken away right here, right now, right before my eyes. What kind of God would allow such a thing to happen?" The last thing I remember before I hobbled over to the hospital chapel, to sob like a baby—and plead with the Creator to take me instead—was witnessing two ICU doctors and two critical care nurses each take a corner of Alena's wheeled gurney so they could all run like the wind in unison down that long unforgiving hallway to catch the next elevator up to the 3rd floor ICU. I had never seen four human beings run so bloody fast in all my life.

Did I mention that I cried? Boy, did I ever cry. I cried inconsolably for several hours in that spiritually vacuous chapel—and again upstairs in that most inhospitable respite room just outside the ICU. Yes it was true Alena was still very much alive, and now under the exceptional care of some of the best clinicians in the world. Yes it was true Marianne would soon be here at my side. Yes it was true Megan was feeling much better—safe at home, snug as a bug in a rug. But unlike Alena, there would be no mommy for me to cry out to—and no protective father figure to step forward to save the day. There really never was, was there? Drenched in tears, I was relegated to the desolate realm of that comatose baby girl from Boston Bar and those two precious little toddlers from Lions Bay. I was laid bare and cast asunder in some sterile medical facility full of clanging noise and plundered flesh. My own personal cold case—the one that I'd been working on for 52 years—had finally been solved. My autopsy was complete and a report was forthcoming. It was indeed the end of my beginning. The truth about my hidden childhood and my desperate gasp-for-air drowning in 1965 had been jiggled loose. So many other painful memories had been wrenched to the surface too. But what I didn't know—and what I couldn't possibly understand at the time—was that my ensuing 10-year quest to hunt down and capture the eerie likeness of my killer—in order to win her everlasting praise and affection—would once again be the very death of me. I would soon be on my knees again, pleasing and showing some incarnate avatar just how sorry I was for being so very bad. At least that would be the lingo she would insist I use in order to give her exactly what she needed—and just *had* to have.

All that seed-planted damage of myocarditis from 1977—together with the accumulated effects of far too much alcohol survival escapism in the 2010s—would soon quietly inflict me with a silent killer known as atrial fibrillation. Without my knowledge, the efficacy of the left side of my heart muscle would slowly drop to 50 percent. Without any outward symptoms, tiny uncirculated pools of blood in my left atrium would progressively coagulate into hundreds of Costco-sized blood clots. Without any warning, one of those clots would eventually break loose and strike me down with a massive stroke and a calamitous tumble in front of a speeding BMW on a busy street in downtown Victoria. Yes, that's right. On January 5, 2017, I too would be fighting for my life in the ICU. I too would be under the intense care of world-class clinicians. I too would have teary loved ones at my side. For several hours I would be rendered completely blind, unable to speak, and full left-side hemiplegic. I would be 59 years old. But for the miracle of an endovascular thrombectomy catheter intervention—administered in the neurotrauma room at Victoria General Hospital—I would most certainly have spent my remaining days as a virtual vegetable in a COVID-vulnerable nursing home. It would be yet another time when I would yet again have to confront the sudden jolt of imminent death—traceable all the way back with irrefutable bread-crumb evidence to the rank barbarity of you know who. My last visual recollection as a living, breathing human being would have been the front licence plate of that thunderous German import screeching to a fucking halt just inches from my face.

So if you think what you've read so far has been just about as intense as it could ever be, think again. I suggest you get a bigger boat. You thought there was unbridled excess and wild incandescent sex back in the 1970s? Well I'm here to tell you straight up that all those primitive disco-dancing neanderthals were rank amateurs. As that Captain Sully guy would say, "brace for impact." My relentless quest for self-destruction would soon push me to the very brink of unimaginable success. Frothing with 52 years of finally unleashed rage, I would soon be elected by all my peers in business as President of the Institute of Certified Management Consultants of British Columbia. I would soon be serving on the lofty National Board of Directors at CMC-Canada. I would find myself delivering speeches on business design excellence at innovation conferences down in Fort Lauderdale, and overseas in London. I would soon be awash in silly amounts of money, and spending as much time commuting on Helijet as the Premier and her entire Cabinet. A couple of years in, Tony Parsons of television news broadcasting fame would turn to me on the helicopter and say, "Good to see you, Russ. How's Alena? John Daly told me about her remarkable story of survival. Here's an autographed copy of my book if you think it would help. I've penned a special message in it for her. Please do give Alena my very best."

As Megan would soon learn to say, being called down to HR at my consulting firm would actually mean walking over to Holt Renfrew to pick up my latest Brioni signature suit from the in-store tailor. All the twenty-something servers over at the Italian Kitchen eatery on Alberni Street would soon knick name me R-Money. I would soon start to lose count how many times some love interest with a hyper-erotic libido and a demonstrable personality disorder would take a slow sexy sip of prosecco, unfurl and shake loose her ponytail, toss aside her Max Mara scrunchie, anaesthetize me with that sultry Sienna Miller eye fuck, and quip,

"You know I'm not into girls, right? But Ksenia and I have been talking: you know, the one from yoga with the pink lulus and that really cute tush? Anyway, she and I have a plan. Oh come on, handsome, you know you'd totally be into it. Resos again at the Fairmont in Whistler? No different than our naughty three-way with Jessica from Island Health last September, remember babe?"

So rather than ending up destitute and addicted to heroin in the Downtown Eastside, all my childhood trauma would actually land me Tiffany-twisted in Coal Harbour—addicted to medical merlot and shameless self-promotion. As I might have told Ernest Hemingway, it frankly wouldn't go so well. Like so many other things in my life, I just couldn't find a sensible way to bury the lead. These were an innocent child's last moments. I would soon morph from plucky worrywart with the impish allure of Richard Gere to raving asshole looking to make the entire world pay for what just one person did. My two daughters, Megan and Alena, would be the ones who would end up paying the biggest price. Madness. Such unforgiveable madness.

# PART II:

When an entire country breaks
the soul of innocence ...

**CHAPTER 5:** A Million Miles Away

AS I REFLECT back on my rather extraordinary life, I can say that despite everything I was forced to endure—or did end up enduring because of my own rank stupidity—there were remarkably quite a number of occasions when I did experience what it's truly like to be happy. Despite everything my mother and all those pencil skirts and Ksenias threw my way, there was just something in my nature that allowed me to occasionally catch what Pink Floyd might have said were fleeting, corner-eye glimpses of receding pain. Not one single day goes by where I don't think it probably had something to do with the affectionate presence of Grandpa Fred. There were just things in what he said and did that led me to believe that he thought Grandma Margorie was insane—and that one day his very own daughter would probably come to murder me in my sleep. He never said anything specific, but it's clear to me now he was always trying to give me the heads up. I didn't like the fact that he always referred to black people as darkies, but there was just something about his words that gave me some tiny sense of hope that maybe one day I would be safe. A beleaguered child of two World Wars, Great Depression starvation, and Spanish flu pandemic anguish, he was pretty much resolved to fact that as mere mortals there's really not much we humans can ever do to ward off the forces of darkness. He was the kind of person who always found a way to crack a groaner dad joke—and persevere with regal grace even in the face of unimaginable cruelty and betrayal.

So whether it was the indelible spirit of my Grandpa Fred—or just bone ass luck—I quite often found a way to wallow in quiet contemplation and warm reflection with nature. Taking long slow walks in the forest—or strolling along a secluded sandy beach— have always been my way of catching glimpses of emotional calm. As silly as it may sound, I was once blessed with the chance to watch a playful purring kitten pounce on a ball of wool on the dining room floor as the theme from *A Summer Place* played softly in the background. I'm pretty sure it was 1961. I once rode my bicycle over to Becker's so I could buy red licorice and hold hands with a pretty girl in Grade 3. I know for sure it was 1965. It's what prompted my drowning later in the day. On my *Toronto Star* newspaper route the year before, I regularly got to collect from Mr. Bathgate up the street. He was that star NHL right winger who scored the winning goal in the 1963 Stanley Cup Final. He always gave me a whopping $1 tip and once even allowed me to take a sneak peek at all the topless honeys diving in and out of his backyard pool. As a globe-trotting lawman and keynote-speaking consultant, I certainly got to witness more than my fair share of resplendent sunrises over the Atlantic Ocean, that's for sure. Back in the early 1990s I of course got to hold two tiny newborns in my arms in the maternity ward, and watch as their angelic mother told them just how very much they would always be loved. In 2001, I had the pleasure of taking a future Cactus Club executive to a tween hip-hop class on a snowy Saturday morning while hung over—after my evening out with double Black Russians. In 2007, I got to watch my youngest absolutely nail the role of Juliet in the high school play. Even as a homicide investigator in the late 1980s—heading with great dispatch to every remote corner of British Columbia—not one single week ever went by without there being yet another opportunity for me to ride like a charmed rockstar in a Citation jet or a twin-engine King Air over all of the majestic mountains, sweeping boreal forest valleys, and meandering rivers that come together with such elaborate-ballet precision to make this province the most beautiful place on earth.

There is no denying that through my short, 13-year marriage to Marianne I was able to experience degrees of gentle intimacy and untroubled peace the likes of which I'm sure even Wordsworth and Yeats would have found hard to quantify with simple words and poetic prose. That five years she and I spent together in our first home in the tranquil seaside community of Steveston just south of Vancouver certainly stands out for me as a time when I enjoyed no end of simple pleasure and tender romance. It's the place where we welcomed our firstborn child into this world—and awkwardly wall-papered our first nursery. It's where we first learned to curse IKEA for the grand stupidity of all their furniture assembly instructions. It's where we hosted our first wine and Pictionary night with that couple from the office that nobody could ever stand. It's where we brought home and proudly displayed our very first slow cooker from Rival. While Marianne had been rendered occasionally wary of the external universe after her tiny 1982 Honda Civic was T-boned by that gargantuan Coca-Cola delivery truck at the nearby Safeway, it was really a time and place where our biggest worry was whether we had paired the poached salmon with the correct Chablis—and whether *Knots Landing* would be preempted tonight by some stupid hockey game. It was the late 1980s. As Wordsworth might have said, it was "when meek aspirations and sage content would absolve me of afflictions strange."

But despite all these many wonderful things, there was really only one time in my life when I felt sustained happiness might finally be within reach. It was the summer 1978. I had fully recovered from my anorexia nervosa and scurvy, and all the clumps of head hair that had fallen out following that gruesome double autopsy were slowly growing back. I was still reeling somewhat from the recent torching of my police cruiser by that scumbag who didn't take kindly to me stumbling across his hash lab—when I was dispatched Code 3 to his shithole apartment to save his common law wife from having to undergo yet another intimate partner beating. But hey, I was 21 years old and in great physical shape. I was full of piss and vinegar and ready to take on the world. I had decent coin in my pocket and a great first-responder constable job with the RCMP. I had a brandnew Chevy truck with one of those newfangled cassette players from Pioneer.

God damn it, I even had my own cosey little rental apartment over on East 15th Street directly across the road from Lions Gate Hospital. You can draw your own smarty pants conclusions as to why I chose to live so close to the morgue over there, but let's just say after witnessing those two horrifically burnt girls carved up with scalpels and oscillating saws—and partitioned into jars and beakers—it was just something I felt very obligated to do.

So here I was living the French Foreign Legion dream in what clearly has to be the most picturesque urban neighbourhood in the world outside of Monaco. The patrol zone to which I was assigned by the RCMP that summer was what all you young whippersnappers today call Lower Lonsdale. Back then we knuckle-dragging neanderthal police officers simply called it City South. It was the downtown core of the largely middleclass City of North Vancouver. It was an action-packed playground of uniformed cop patrol bounded by Victoria Park to the north, Mosquito Creek marina to the west, the Saskatchewan wheat pool terminals to the east, and Burrard Inlet and the Pacific Ocean to the south. Perched with architectural precision on a steep incline, the views of Mount Baker and the downtown Vancouver skyline were simply stunning. Being posted as an RCMP officer in 1978 to the City South precinct house of North Vancouver Detachment was akin to a Chicago beat cop being transferred to Waikiki Beach. It was pure urban policework heaven. The surrounding Vancouver region was affectionally called Lotus Land by all the locals because it was considered to be such a laid back paradise of playful dialectic and sensual narcotic consumption. When I first heard about it, I half expected to find citizens wandering the streets wearing graceful flowing togas and wreath headdresses made of bright lavender flower pedals. Being a typical white privilege dumbass from Toronto, I was of course completely unaware that right under my sanctimonious Canadian nose—over in the far western corner of the patrol zone—was a patch of cultural genocide enslavement known as the Mission Indian Reserve No. 1 where as far back as the 1890s innocent human beings from the Squamish Nation had been rounded up like livestock and housed against their will in colonial-oppression homes so that they could be stripped of all their language and culture, and forced to send their children to a nearby internment school where they would be subjected to no end of criminal violence, malnutrition and sexual defilement. It would be 44 years before I would come to realize with eternal shame that every day on patrol I always drove right past what was essentially the scene of normalized desecration—and a waystation to the Downtown Eastside. Sometime in 1978 I realized RCMP Special Constable Teddy Seward—who was assigned to City South as our lone Indigenous liaison officer—had always been called "the FBI" not because he walked and talked like a G-Man, but because he was being smeared as a "Fucking Big Indian."

When I was first assigned to City South right of out of the training academy in Regina I was told by all the racist and misogynistic blokes on my watch—in other words by absolutely everybody with whom I worked—that this would be the ideal place for a young buck like myself to cut his teeth and make his way in this man's army. They stressed that not only was this the most action packed patrol zone at the detachment, it was also a bustling slice of city life that was replete with trendy nightclubs, exotic stripper bars, and to-die-for steak and lobster joints. They went out of their way to stress that the local population here was primarily composed of burly fishermen, pot-head loggers, beer-guzzling pipefitter welders from the local shipyards, and most importantly in their estimation: lonely apartment-dwelling single women in their twenties who listen to Air Supply and commute daily to dreary downtown Vancouver office jobs in skirts and heels—looking to bag themselves a decent husband who didn't smell like fish, weed or beer. I was told to not underestimate the power of the RCMP uniform and the globally revered Mountie brand. It was their assertion that all the local ladies—what they called talent—were forever afflicted by scarlet fever. It took me awhile, but I finally clued in that they were trying to say this would be the ideal place for a 21-year-old man like me to meet a nice girl and get married. It took me even longer, but I also eventually figured out that scarlet fever was a crude misogynistic reference to the red serge uniform we wore on parade—something they said women found simply irresistible. Always a carryover from the pig-male 1950s, it was just how members of the RCMP viewed the world. Helen who worked the switchboard would always go out of her way to remind me that Bishops up at 16th and Lonsdale was the best place to snag a discount on an engagement ring. She never missed a chance to drop the hint that her lovely daughter Debbie was single, and not doing anything this weekend.

So while all this jibber-jabber about rousing cop action and captive females seemed to amuse everyone else, it wasn't really who I was as a person. I learned very early on that, as it relates to my time in the RCMP, I would always be considered the white sheep of the family. I particularly had a hard time embracing the Mountie lingo that was in such wide use back then. People who committed crimes were said to be shit rats. Troubled folks with mental health and addiction issues were dismissed as being hypes. Anybody who didn't completely agree with the police on social-justice issues was to be arrested under the "stunned cunts act." Female RCMP officers were simply called Wrens, which I initially thought was a polite reference to the critical role women played in winning World War II. It actually meant "wasted regimental number." All bowel movements on duty were said to be "giving birth to a lawyer." When flirting with all the young girls at the Catholic high school up on Keith Road all the old-timer constables would say, "If they're old enough to set the table, they're old enough to eat." If you did someone a big favour, they'd say, "That was mighty white of you, ass wipe." Hair and fiber particles collected from the underwear of sobbing rape victims were to be called "kitty litter." If you refused to play golf or drink room temperature beer that tasted like horse urine you were labelled a faggot, a homo, a fudge packer and a bone smoker. It was really nothing short of brutal. Back in the day comedians would jest that high school shop class was the place where hope and inspiration would go to die. Well, I found out firsthand that, in the 1970s, policework was the place where bitter incels would go to flourish—and stew in all their don't-ever-fuck-with-us brethren.

So the real reason why the summer of 1978 stands out for me as a time when it appeared as though sustained happiness might finally be within reach was because it was the beginning of a 10-month stretch when—for the very first time ever—I experienced what it was like to have unfettered personal freedom and the ability to set the pace and soft tempo of my very own life. Every night when I went out on patrol I was empowered by my watch commanders and my patrol sergeants to make pretty much whatever sensible decision I thought was appropriate. Nobody ever dressed me down in front of the gang—or scolded me for not measuring up. Nobody ever said, "Come here, stupid." As I drove from dispatched call to dispatched call I often felt like one of those nostalgic Hallmark card characters with a wintry toque and a long flowing scarf, skating alone on a frozen pond in a secluded countryside meadow with only gentle moonlight to guide his way. With every firm yet silent thrust of my patrol car, I glided along sweeping-vista streets with pleasing ease, sensing no end of safety and inner peace. There wasn't a single bathroom sink or Holiday Inn balcony anywhere to be found. I almost always took my 2:00 a.m. meal break at Delo's Place at the foot of Lonsdale, down by those creosote-soaked pylons holding up that rickety old wooden pier. They made the very best baked lasagna in town, and being so close to all those pipefitter welders from the shipyards across the street made me feel like I was part of something meaningful and industrious. For the first time in my life, I felt like I was making a demonstrable difference in this world; that I mattered, that I belonged. Saying "morning, Mack" and "have a good one, Bill" made me feel like I was part of a functional loving family composed of nice people who actually knew who I was—who actually liked me. These men cussed and cursed like there was no tomorrow, but God help you if you ever disrespected a woman or talked shit about any person of colour. Those were fighting words, don't you know.

At home on my days off I almost always treated myself to my favourite delicacy meal of fried porkchops with cream of mushroom soup sauce, paired with minute rice and two beers. I almost always sat alone on the couch in the dark watching Johnny Carson or the movie of the week. With there being only 11 channels to choose from in 1978, there really wasn't much else to watch. It was better than going out to stripper bars, I thought. I was going to meet that other rookie from Capilano zone for a beer at the Legion, but he hurt his back tussling with unworthy Order of Canada recipient Bobby Hull at an intimate partner violence call up near Handsworth Secondary School and had to cancel. By 1979, I became a huge fan of all the progressive rock being played by that new FM station known as CFOX. I would spend hours sitting in the dark listening to the likes of Pink Floyd, Fleetwood Mac, Bob Seger and The Eagles. It was a welcome reprieve from all those sex-slave reverberations of 1970s disco. Immersing myself in the gentle warmth of all their poetic lyrics allowed me to become even more detached from the outside world—and embrace the reality I was now no longer a heartsick teenager. In the shower in the morning I would often sing, "As I walked into Delo's restaurant, strung out from the road, I could the feel the eyes upon me. Thank God I'm finally old." I still woke up at 3:10 a.m. to scan the bedroom for the approach of you-know-who. I still placed sneakers at the base of my bed. But here I was finally safe. I was right where I wanted to be, and nobody would ever again come down the hall at night to defile me while daddy and the others slept. Nobody would ever again order me to sit at the bottom of the family stairs so they could repeatedly punch me in the face. Nobody would ever again attempt to murder me in a sink because I was off being who I really was at Becker's eating red licorice with a pretty girl in Grade 3—who actually cared about what I had to say about the world. In 21 years of life, I'd never before known such serene happiness. At age 21, I was ready to caress the affectionate presence of Bob Seger, and just turn the page.

# CHAPTER 6: Three Bravo Two

SO YES, THOSE were just some of the memories of 1978 upon which I reflected as I sat motionless beside Alena in that darkened negative pressure room upstairs in the ICU on the rainy evening of November 6, 2009. It was a moment like no other. I was heartened Alena was doing better. It was 11:45 p.m. and she had been here fully sedated for about five hours. She was essentially unconscious, but we never did have to follow through with intubation. She was under the constant one-on-one attention of her assigned critical care nurse, Liz. Every once and awhile one or more ICU doctors would pop in and out, making slow adjustments to her infusion flow after one or more of her patient monitor screens set off some sort of alarm. Her bloating was starting to recede, and she was breathing with greater ease. She still had that God awful tube protruding from her chest—and many more butterfly ports from her arms—but all and all she seemed to be responding well to treatment. All of this was encouraging to say the very least, but I was totally exhausted and emotionally drained. I was convinced there wasn't a single tear left inside my head. I was still being reminded every hour that it may take several days for any of us to know if Alena would survive. I was told that her lab tests had confirmed the presence of both H1N1 and streptococcal toxic shock syndrome—or what Liz and Dr. Grant kept referring to as TSS. I was told her medical condition was so distressing that even hospital CEO Dianne Doyle had been put on notice. Within just a few short hours, Alena's chart was the talk of almost every ward at St. Paul's. News of that precious 16-year-old girl up in the ICU clinging to life with TSS sent chills down the backs of even some the most seasoned clinicians.

Being so worried and feeling so helpless about everything of course took me back to all those please-help-me-understand memories of Grandpa Fred. He never had any answers, but he always knew just what to say. Watching Alena purr like a little kitten just now of course took me back to all those fleeting glimpse recollections of receding pain I was so lucky to experience at various different stages of my turbulent life. With Marianne's flight from Toronto set to land at YVR in about an hour, all of those memories of our simple life together in our first home in Steveston also came flooding back. But it was the calm and nurturing bedside manner of Nurse Liz, combined with the tranquil silence and dark lighting of that isolation room—blended in with the mood-calming rain just outside Alena's window—that took me back to that peaceful place in City South where, for the first time, I felt like I might actually have a chance to live out the modest life of an ordinary man—free of withering affection and unimaginable cruelty.

When another one of Alena's screeching noise alarms went off I was immediately jolted back into present moment reality. With Liz and Dr. Wong scurrying over to see what the heck was the matter, it was like being awakened from one of those deep, pleasant-thought dreams at night by some unexpected loud noise, only to find that when you drift back to sleep you can't ever seem to reacquire the thread. As I continued to sit quietly in my corner chair, I tried hard to reestablish my soothing recollection of 1978—and what The Eagles would surely have said was my peaceful easy feeling union with resplendent serenity. But it was to no avail. The thread was lost. As I tried harder to get it back— and as Liz and the good doctor continued to scurry and fuss—I was dragged kicking and screaming by my hippocampus right back to the spring of 1979. I was yanked abruptly to the exact moment in time when my exposure to safety and serenity came to a sudden screeching noise halt on April 14, 1979. From that exact moment, 30 years earlier, I would never again feel comfortably settled in my skin. I would never again live and breathe without some underlying notion of fear and loathing slowly eating away at my inner soul. I would be issued a first-class ticket to Caligula, and be the first one to always choose debauchery and extravagance over common sense and self-respect. Within six months I would be having a fling with a perfidious nymphomaniac who spoke of nothing but cocaine and lewd threesomes with her best friend Amy from ballet class. It was the exact date in 1979 when yet another psychotic female—no relation to my mother—just up and attempted to murder me. I was on duty and in uniform at the time, and although I tried my best to brush it off in front of the guys as just another episode of rousing cop action, it had a profoundly catastrophic effect on my psyche and how I interacted with the surrounding universe. Until earth angel Marianne came along in 1985, my life would be defined by a steady stream of chaos, heartache and erotic indulgence—particularly with women who would always accompany their initial sip of dessert wine and mango-raspberry sorbet with the perfunctory phrase, "I love my husband, but this is just something I need." Later in the parking lot of the restaurant—or in the elevator heading up with reckless abandon to my apartment—they would often add, "You're good with anal, right?"

"Three Bravo Two, North Van, copy a call?"

Yup, that was indeed how it all began. It was the radio call I received from the dispatcher at North Vancouver RCMP Detachment at 2:25 a.m. on the morning of April 14, 1979. Three Bravo Two was the call sign for my police cruiser for that particular nightshift. It was a shift that had commenced two hours earlier at 12:00 a.m. As always I was on routine patrol in City South, but the thing that made this one slightly different was the fucked up fact that I had been saddled by my watch commander with an unarmed ride-along dude by the name of Auxiliary Constable Van Born. He was a good guy I guess, but his 6' 7" presence in uniform in my car was cramping my style. With his imposing size—and my baby-faced complexion—the citizens with whom we were about to interact tonight would most likely assume he was the actual cop and me, well, I'd be seen as the jackass student ride along with no real relevance. I would have to spend my entire nightshift convincing crooks and complainants to pay attention to me, not him. This was my constructed reality, and I didn't take lightly to it being fucked with.

"North Van, Three Bravo Two, go ahead."

Yup, that's how I responded as I pulled over to jot down the details of the location to which I was about to be dispatched. Soon enough I learned it was a no biggie. No biggie at all. I was to head on over to 377 East 2nd Street, just a few blocks east of Lonsdale in order to sort out some sort of argument between a MacLure's cab driver and a woman he'd just picked up from the hooker stroll over on Hornby Street in downtown Vancouver. Upon our arrival there the driver explained that the woman never returned to his cab to pay her $13 fare after she said she needed to pop up to her apartment to get her wallet. It was the classic taxi-no-pay case, similar to what all you food-service jockeys call a dine-and-dash. I figured I'd do a little Russ Grabb sweet talking and be outta there lickety-split in less than 10 minutes. I figured wrong.

As the cabbie, Auxiliary Constable Van Born and I walked up to the door of the woman's apartment she graciously opened it up and invited us all in without any argument. Initially she was surprisingly polite and quite talkative. She looked to be in her late twenties and was nicely dressed for a person of her socio-economic footing. I made small talk with her about the requirement to pay up. I scanned the joint to look for any signs of danger. There was nothing to worry about from a first-responder cop point of view, but the place was God-awful dirty. I was pretty certain she was a neophyte hoarder with complete indifference to the smell of feces, urine and vomit. Most disturbing for me at least was the fact that the tea towel she had hanging off the front of her stove wasn't folded exactly symmetrical. I made a mental note to myself to sleathfully walk over and straighten it once this little fracas had been cleared up, and the driver was well on his way with his precious money—all fucking $13 of it.

As I continued to chit chat with the woman—and tactfully nudge her toward the notion of settling up so we could all be on our way—it became increasingly clear that something was weirdly different about her. She wasn't drunk. She wasn't high. Clearly she was a bit mentally unstable, but there had to be something else. Then it hit me. It hit me right after she started talking about our upcoming federal election, and whether President Jimmy Carter would—in her learned opinion—be a far better choice for Canada than what she described as that pussy, Joe Clark or that fucking fag, Pierre Elliott Trudeau. It hit me instantly that she was just lonely. Plain and simple, she just wanted sensory feedback that she mattered, that she belonged, that she was valued and appreciated, and that maybe—just maybe—one day she would be loved for who she really was as a person. Not paying her taxi fare was just her ruse to have a bunch of humans drop by so she wouldn't once again have to stare at that vial of barbiturates on her kitchen counter, and fight back all those terrible ideations of suicide. She was dying inside and her searing pain was pouring out through her pores. Her quest for validation and interpersonal relevance was overtaking everything. I'm not sure how I arrived at this psychiatric analysis so quickly, but anyhoo, it was all about to go terribly sideways when fuck stick cabbie boy started getting antsy and insisting upon prompt payment.

"North Van, Three Bravo Two, 10-33."

Yup, that was the radio call I made after the woman didn't take so well to being told by antsy boy to hurry up and pay—and to having all her personal validation time cut so short. It prompted her to throw a crumpled $10 bill his way, and to punch him just as hard as she could in the mouth. It prompted me to ask Auxiliary Constable Van Born to escort the driver outside so he could give his statement and leave. It prompted her to start screaming, "How dare you, how fucking dare you? Who are you people? Who the fuck are you? Don't you know? Don't you understand? Where's your fucking soul?" To any other human this would have come across as the ramblings of a raving lunatic. To me, it was all very familiar. I could totally relate. I tried to reassure her that the driver had overstepped—and that I'd be happy to stay and chat—but it was too late. It escalated with her throwing a wild punch at me, knocking my police notebook over onto the floor. When I bent down to pick it up I felt this creepy shewsh sound beside my right jugular vein. When I looked up to see what it was, I saw that she had just come at me with an ominous 8" butcher knife. It had narrowly missed my throat by just a tiny hair.

"Three Bravo Two, North Van, say again, over."

That was the dispatcher responding back, not really sure if I had actually just called in a 10-33: the rarely used police code for "officer needs assistance, send back up immediately." Grabbing my notebook with my left hand, I quickly stood upright—and as I did so, I drew my police revolver from the holster on my right side. I pointed the gun at the woman and yelled, "Drop the knife, or I'll shoot." She yelled back, "If I'm going to die, I may as well take a fucking pig with me." She lunged at me again with the knife. This time she had an empty beer bottle in her other hand. As she madly swung and flailed away at me, I quickly backed up against the inside surface of the hallway the door. Trapped alone with her inside that dark apartment, I continued to point my gun and yell, "You're under arrest, stop or I'll shoot, stop or I'll shoot."

"North Van, Three Bravo Two, 10-33, suspect with knife."

That was me clarifying that I wasn't fucking kidding. I was scared shitless. If she lunged at me again, I would have to kill her in self defence, or end up dead myself. Back at the training academy we had all been told that there's no such thing as wounding somebody in the leg, and that any North American police officer who had ever been dumb enough to try it, had always ended up dead with a knife stuck in his eye socket. Back in those Jurassic policing days we had no pepper spray, no baton, no taser, no bean-bag gun, no body armour, no body cam, no dash-cam video, no 9mm automatic pistol, no Air 1 helicopter, and no fucking carbine rifle. Back in the day we just did policework. All we had was a six-shot 38-special revolver, a set of handcuffs, a clunky portable radio, and the gift of the gab. But there would be no Russ Grabb sweet talking this time around. This was life and death. Ya, for fucking reals, dude. For reals.

"All units, North Van. Officer needs immediate assistance 377 East 2nd, apartment 5. All units City South, City North, Lynn Valley and Pemberton, respond Code 3. Capilano stand by."

With Auxiliary Constable Van Born still outside with the cabbie—and with back up still on its way—I figured the smart move here would be to simply re-holster my weapon and wait. After all, the woman had just retreated somewhat into her galley kitchen with knife in hand. There was no point taking a human life simply because I had more than enough grounds to do so under the law. This was North Vancouver 1979, not Edmundston, 2020. Hoping for the best I kept calm and stood silent as she picked up the wall-mounted telephone and spoke briefly to her lawyer, Brian Coleman. I could have fled from her place at this point, but that would have created an untenable armed-and-barricaded situation. It would have been 24 hours before any adequately equipped ERT could be deployed. Who knows what she would have done to herself or someone else in the meantime.

"Three Bravo Two, North Van, status update."

There was no time at this stage to give a status update. As all the backup officers came barreling through the door, the woman once again became noticeably agitated and aggressive. She ran out from behind the kitchen counter and kicked a dining room chair into my shins. As I winced with pain she came at me again with the knife and beer bottle. Reacting instinctively to my self-defence training from Regina I blocked her final knife thrust with my left forearm and aggressively applied a painful tiger claw clutch to her trachea, pushing her up against her dining room wall as hard as I could. As I pinned her 6" off the ground against the wall, with her feet dangling, the backup members rushed over, grabbed the knife and flung her onto the floor. When we got her back to the detachment cellblock she was so violent and angry she had to be restrained twice in a straitjacket borrowed from Lions Gate Hospital across the street. We were all shocked to learn that she was on probation at the time for kidnapping, use of an offensive weapon, and possession of stolen property in Vancouver—the conditions of which were for her to abstain from drugs and alcohol and to undergo psychiatric treatment. The C-237 crime report signed by Inspector Davis said that I'd received a minor cut to the side of my neck, but trying not to piss off all the attention hounds on my watch, and worried about all the cookies I might get from Helen and Debbie, I simply brushed that off as a fishing accident.

On May 2, 1979, stunned readers of the *North Shore News* would read that 27-year-old Rose Ann McKay—also known as Rose Ann Dercach—was currently out on bail after having been charged in North Vancouver Provincial Court with the attempted murder of Constable Russell George Grabb in Lower Lonsdale on April 14, 1979. Had she been successful in slicing my throat that night, my last visual recollection as a living, breathing human being would have been the sight of that crooked tea towel hanging off the front of that kitchen stove. It was the second time in 21 years of life where I had been forced to confront the sudden jolt of imminent death—with my 1965 drowning of course being the first. As I reflected upon this episode into the summer of 1979, it dawned on me that this was also the second time a woman had tried to murder me after I had done my level best to be nice to her—and win her trust and admiration. As an adolescent with a gun and a broken heart, I soon became one hell of a fucked up human being. No amount of remarkable success inside the RCMP—or later in business consulting—would ever make any difference. As I say, one hell of a fucked up human being. For reals.

Never reported by the mainstream media was the fact that on April 22, 1979—exactly two weeks after my encounter with Rose Ann McKay—she was found to be one of seven crooks who were seated in a stolen Lincoln Continental with Texas licence plates when it was pulled over for speeding by the RCMP in the nearby City of Burnaby. Like a bloodcurdling scene from a classic Joseph Wambaugh novel, one of the male occupants of that stolen car—a bank robber out on parole—exited the vehicle and summarily gunned down RCMP Constable John Buis and Constable Jack Robinson. It prompted a massive shootout and a sidewalk hostage-taking stand off the likes of which Burnaby had never before seen. Luckily, both officers survived their wounds, but 43 years later John Buis would still be undergoing painful surgeries to repair the horrific tissue damage inflicted upon his right leg that day by that sawed-off shotgun. Although Rose Ann just sat there silently, and calmy watched all of this gunplay unfold right before her eyes, it's worth noting that the very next day—yes, on April 23, 1979—she ended up in Lions Gate Hospital in grave condition after she tried to kill herself with that vial of barbiturates that I'd seen calling out her name—and staring her down at her apartment, back on April 14, 1979. In November of 1984—going by the name of Rose Ann Dercach—she would be rearrested in Toronto for stabbing and nearly killing a man she'd met in a bar. Having served a jail term for her vicious attack, she would die in September of 1987, but not before being diagnosed by the Clarke Institute with a borderline personality disorder, a history of severe childhood sex abuse, and a manifest hatred of any man who ever attempted to extend her thoughtful compassion. It later came out that when John and Jack were so viciously gunned down, Rose Ann had been packing a small calibre handgun that she tossed under the Lincoln before more backup arrived.

So ya, this was the batshit crazy thing about which I was daydreaming when Marianne arrived at the ICU at 1:15 a.m. It was of course now the early morning of November 7, 2009. As I greeted her at the reception desk—way down the ward from Alena—I was enveloped by a warm sense of calm. She was the earth angel who I loved more than anything else in this world, but because I was so terribly afflicted with shame for everything I had done—and all the hurt that I had caused—I felt it would be wrong of me to ever again try to act upon those feelings. Marianne had long since re-partnered—and was living far away in Ottawa—so it probably wasn't going to be something that could ever be pursued in any event. I shook her hand, gave her a big hug and said, "I'm so glad you're here. Oh man, what a day. Follow me and I'll take you to Alena's room. She's doing better now, but she's still in critical condition. She's sedated, so we'll have to be very quiet." Marianne smiled softly and said, "Okay, honey, I understand."

When we entered Alena's negative pressure room all of her vitals were still showing on the monitors as being very close to the danger zone. One alarm in particular kept pinging, so we had to wait for Liz to work her magic before we could approach. As Marianne got closer to Alena she said, "Hi, honey." Within seconds Alena's racing heartrate started to slow. Almost immediately her low blood pressure started to rise and normalize. Almost on cue, her oxygen sats started to rise. Suddenly she had a normal respiration rate, and all of the patient monitor screens stopped pinging alarms. Every clinician head in the ICU turned to see what the heck was making such a breakthrough science difference. Alena opened her eyes slowly and said, "Hi, mommy." Well needless to say, there were indeed more tears left inside my head. What a scene. What a sight. Earth angel Marianne was here, and everything was now going to be okay. It would be nine more days of worry, but Alena would finally turn the corner and go home to convalesce in her own bed in her own jammy jams. Marianne would have to return to Ottawa for now, but under the close watchful eye of me and Megan—and her new beau, Luke—Alena would go on to make a full recovery over the next three, rather commendable years. Somehow she would find a way to persevere with regal grace and endearing humour even in the face of such imaginable hardship. She never met her Great Grandpa Fred, but she sure enough knew exactly what he would have expected her to have done under such harrowing circumstances. She was—and would always remain—that shining example model to whom I would always look up whenever I was wanting for hope and inspiration. She would always hate me for saying so, but she will always remain my special little peanut. There would be times when she would fall to such great depths of despair for all that happened to her back in 2009—and how I turned into such an angry thrash-about asshole—but inch by inch she would eventually come to realize just how deeply she was loved and admired by everyone. Oh Alena, I am just so sorry. So very sorry. To my dying day, I will do everything I can to fix what I so horribly broke.

As I was lying in bed exhausted on the morning of Tuesday, November 10, 2009, I said to myself, holy fuck this was fucking huge. Over the past few days, I had watched my youngest daughter almost die right before my eyes. That in turn forced me to relive my 1965 drowning and revisit every dark corner and recess of my barbaric childhood. That in turn triggered all those flashbacks of dead and dying children from my time with the RCMP. The final domino of course was having to rehash everything that happened with Rose Ann McKay—and how all that affected me and John Buis for what seemed like an eternity. Truth be told, the hardest thing was witnessing my special girl Marianne once again slip away—and fly off to Ottawa for what would feel like an even longer eternity. I remember thinking to myself, how the crap am I ever going to recover from any of this? Just the sight of TSS-ravaged skin peeling away from Alena's palms was enough to make me triple my wine intake. Conventional wisdom says you're supposed to talk it out, but who the heck was ever going to listen to little old Russ Grabb?

For more than a decade after Alena was discharged from St. Paul's, both she and Megan would constantly ride my ass for incessantly wanting to chat about the events of November 6, 2009. I couldn't blame them, really. After all, this was Alena's near death experience, not mine. Who was I to say when the time would be right to broach such a delicate subject? My role as the dad was to simply clutch my pearls at the hospital and go home and make spaghetti for the troops when it was all over. My role was not to insert myself into someone else's trauma. How selfish would that be? For Alena and Megan, it was starting to come across as if I were trying to hijack Alena's ordeal in order to draw attention over to myself. But what the two of them never really understood—and couldn't possibly ever know—was that this wasn't just about Alena's frightening brush with death. There were so many other layers to this. It would take the catastrophic global events of 2020—and my harrowing battle with leukemia right in the middle of the first devastating wave of COVID-19—for the two of them to finally realize that November 6, 2009, was actually the chance intersection of multiple jaw-dropping stories of human struggle and survival. As time progressed, Alena and Megan would eventually come to realize that—all things considered—that date in human history was actually the mother of all triggering events for a little guy who had suffered so greatly as a child. Not lost on me was the heart-melting reality that in May of 2020, it would be 28-year-old aspiring med student Alena who would drive her dad to and from chemo every day—and hold his tiny hand as he struggled to get in and out of the car. It would be 30-year-old restaurant ace Megan who would step up and declare, "We will always protect you, Daddy." It would be earth angel Marianne who would tuck me in at night—and tell me just how very much I would always be loved.

For me, this whole Rose Ann McKay and Three Bravo Two saga doesn't just end with her death in Toronto in 1987. Also never reported by the mainstream media was the stunning fact that 18 years after two violent criminals had tried to murder me and John Buis—just two weeks and 11 miles apart—he and I would be standing side-by-side on national television trying our very best as two police spokespersons to explain the inexplicable and defend the indefensible. Yup, it's true. You just can't make this shit up.

Let's just look at the optics here.

Prior to this national media relations assignment related to the 1997 APEC conference in Vancouver, John and I had never before worked together in any capacity. We may have said hello to each other once or twice in 18 years—while passing in some detachment hallway—but we never once ever mutually discussed our two separate attempted murder cases. We never once made small talk about the weather or the Canucks hockey team. We were simply too busy doing our job and keeping Canadians safe.

We didn't have time to engage in the kind of self-aggrandization that all of those tone deaf politicians back in Ottawa seem to relish. In fact, the only case of this nature that I ever really talked about was that incident where my troopmate Constable Rocky Clelland came very close to being killed on duty when he was shot in the back with a high-powered rifle at that prolonged standoff at Gustafsen Lake back in 1995. Of course I also thought a lot about that female member, Constable Candace Smith, who was just a week behind me at the training academy, who'd been shot twice at close range and gravely wounded in 1978 in Brandon, Manitoba by a couple of car thieves—just five weeks after she'd graduated.

But here we were—two hapless shmucks who had been willing to lay down their lives in 1979 in order to uphold the law—now being asked in 1997 to explain to Peter Mansbridge and the Canadian people why Prime Minister Jean Chretien had just ordered the RCMP to crush dissent, and summarily suppress all of the democratic protests being lawfully conducted by a bunch of law-abiding college students over at the nearby UBC school of law. Even harder for us to have to address with the media was the fact that the Prime Minister had done this while he was on his way over from YVR in a bullet-proof limo to have poached salmon and Chablis with two murderous dictators on the peace-loving campus of a major Canadian university.

Are we thinking about the optics here?

Completely missed by the mainstream media and the sanctimonious Canadian people on this glorious APEC conference occasion was the reality that while two decent police officers almost died back in 1979—doing what was best for Canada—blueblood cocksuckers from the Rideau Club back east were then glossing over the cultural genocide provisions of the *Indian Act*, turning a blind eye to the murderous operations of residential schools, and scheming how they might one day misappropriate $60 million in sponsorship funds for naked political gain.

Also completely missed by everyone was the reality that these same two police officers were now the very two saps who would now be asked by this very same Laurentian elite culture to clean up this naked suppression of human rights and lawful dissent— and put pretty pink lipstick on an APEC pepper spray pig. I'm pretty sure I once saw John tear up off camera. We both felt so much shame. I eventually got us out of this debacle by repeating the talking point, "The RCMP wants the same two things as the students: for all the facts to come out and for the Force to be accountable for its actions." As reflected in Hansard, Deputy Prime Minister Herb Gray would build on this clever point when he rose in the House of Commons in 1998 to further defend the indefensible. He specifically mentioned "Sergeant Russ Grabb" by name. Somehow as a knuckle-dragging cop I had learned that the secret to effective communication was not to bash your detractors, but to show where there just might be some common ground. It was a little trick I had learned while sharing baked lasagna at 2:00 a.m. at Delo's Place with a bunch of cop-leery pipefitter welders from the shipyards down in Lower Lonsdale in 1978.

Perhaps everybody overlooked the ugly truth about APEC in 1997 because at that exact moment in time the mainstream media and the sanctimonious Canadian people were too busy fawning over some serial philanderer American President who was putting out the disgusting geezer vibe down in Gastown so he could buy a culturally misappropriated work of Indigenous art for his beret-wearing mistress, Monica Lewinsky, back in Washington, DC. Ya, that's right. Everybody had their eye on the fallacious charm of Bill Clinton, instead of being outraged by the scenes of social injustice being played out nightly on the television news. Nobody of course stopped to ask, "Hey, isn't that John Buis guy that same cop who got blasted with a sawed-off shotgun up on Kingsway in 1979? Isn't Russ Grabb that rookie who almost got his head lopped off with a butcher knife two weeks earlier over in North Van? And how did we all miss the fact that the same violent offender woman was at the scene of both attempted murders?" I guess it makes sense. After all, Gastown was named after an idolized 19th Century pedophile who raped and kept captive a 12-year-old Indigenous girl who would have been in Grade 7 had she been alive when our venerated public education system came of age in the 20th Century.

"Canada, Three Bravo Two, who are you people? Where is your fucking soul, over?"

That was me setting the stage to explain who was to blame, and how it was that an entire community of family members, acquaintances, neighbours, primary school educators and cops from the Chinguacousy Township Police Service in what was then the venerated urban design experiment known as Bramalea could have stood by in the 1960s and done absolutely nothing to stop the unspeakable. That was me bracing you for the reality that, in any situation of abject suffering of the innocent, those to blame are not actually the perpetrators, but rather the blind-eye truth aversionists who we all see in the mirror every morning as we prep to head out and step right over the nearest patch of normalized desecration. I'm talking about a pious group of humans I like to call Canadians. By the time I'm done telling my story you will no doubt come to realize that its terms like venerated, revered and iconic—not evil, monstrous, or repulsive—that betray who is actually behind despicable acts of social injustice and sexual defilement. It's why, in an extended 2019 obituary, the *Vancouver*

*Sun* hero-worshipped wealthy oil tycoon J. Bob Carter as being a savvy, flamboyant and flashy businessman with a checkered past, and a penchant for attracting police and media attention, instead of simply calling him out for being the professed tax evader and convicted child sex offender he really was. This Carter fuck may have been similarly idolized by Peter C. Newman as a "high-flying acquisitor," but it's still true that the two teenage girls upon whom he committed gross indecency were indeed in Grade 9.

# CHAPTER 7: Voices Carry

IT REMINDED ME of that evening in the late 1960s when my father took me to Maple Leaf Gardens to watch the Toronto Maple Leafs battle it out with the Montreal Canadians. I'm talking about that time when he walked me down to ice level before the game so I could shake hands with the very God of NHL hockey himself: No. 4 Jean Beliveau, the iconic Captain of the Montreal Canadians. I was left speechless. I could have sworn he was 7' tall in those skates. It was the biggest—and frankly the only—thrill of my entire childhood. So here I was again in the late summer of 1981: still working as a uniformed first responder at North Vancouver RCMP Detachment, still only 24 years old. I had been sent by my supervisor to the cellblock to check on the sobriety of some prisoner in the drunk tank. Suddenly through the prisoner bay door came the very God of plainclothes homicide investigation: Corporal Fred Maille of what was then known as "E" Division RCMP Serious Crime Section. I of course knew Fred because he had been one of the two homicide investigators who tricked me into being the lead exhibit custodian at the double autopsy of those two little girls who died in that housefire back in 1977. But more than that, Fred had been on the television news every night being showcased to the world as the lead investigator in the kidnapping, torture and murder of 11 children from the Lower Mainland area of British Columbia. It was a still unfolding spree of mass murder that was sending the entire population of Canada into mass panic. When Fred came into the main cellblock area he was in the company of a couple of other homicide investigation legends. They even had Scorsesesque names like Rick Rautio and Eddie Drozda. They were the guys who all starry-eyed RCMP rookies aspired to become. It was like getting to meet Jean Beliveau, Yvan Cournoyer and Dick Duff all at the same time. What an absolute thrill for me: still that plucky little worrywart with a gun doing everything he could to evade his past, and hide deep within elaborate layers of embroidered truth. It was that moment in human history when I now knew exactly what I needed to do. I would continue to work my ass off as a uniformed cop, take night school classes at SFU in criminology and political science—and hopefully one day be drafted to serve as an illustrious homicide investigator at "E" Division RCMP Serious Crime Section. There would be no stopping me. No stopping me at all. Accepting any other fate would be akin to being sent down to the farm team for the 1968 Montreal Canadians as a 4th line scratch.

I guess I should also mention that on this particular occasion in 1981, Fred and the boys had been in the company of some cigar-smoking jackass by the name of Clifford Robert Olson. He was that notorious murderer who would long hold the title as the most prolific serial killer in the history of Canada. At one point he was no more than three feet away from me. They were all here in the cellblock to take a short break from their ongoing tour of the area to locate the bodies of all the still missing children. They had just come down from Whistler where Olson had led them to the remains of 17-year-old Louise Chartrand. Through the small window of that dingy interview room just to the left of the fingerprinting station, I personally witnessed them signing some of the paperwork that formed the basis of their controversial deal to pay Olson $10,000 for each body recovered. It's what prompted me to say to myself, one day I'm going to solve a big cold case murder too—but not unless it's done lawfully by the book, and not unless it also produces some sort of noble downstream benefit for society at large. Little did I know—working right upstairs, right above the cellblock—was then Sergeant Ron MacKay, the psychological profiler whose clever insights 13 years later would put the Green Ribbon Task Force on track to nail Paul Bernardo for the murders of Kristen French and Leslie Mahaffy.

So off I went, working away as a perky first responder in uniform, singularly focused for at least five more years on the goal of one day making it to the big leagues. My first big break came when I was transferred to the major crime section at Richmond Detachment in January of 1986. It was right around the time when Marianne and I became engaged and were settling into our new home in Steveston. It was right after I'd come across the juvenile delinquent son of an RCMP officer arriving at the ER at Richmond General Hospital with a bloody paper plate pressed up against his stomach. When I asked him if I could be of assistance, he removed the plate revealing that he'd been stabbed. It unleashed a couple feet of putrid upper intestine into my hands and onto my crisp RCMP uniform. My quick intervention helped to save his life and catapulted my standing with the local brass. I was put to work a few weeks later in plainclothes running down hot tips on what was then the recent murder of 21-year-old Kim Stolberg at her father's industrial complex up on River Road. What a heartbreaking tragedy that was. On the very night she snuck into her dad's office after hours to plan a surprise anniversary party for her parents, some psycho broke into the place and stabbed her 32 times. My work on that case and another one involving the sexual assault of children committed by a scientist working at the TRIUMF nuclear research facility over at UBC soon put me on the radar with all the mucky mucks downtown. They were particularly gobsmacked by my road trip to Fresno, California to interview one of the children buggered by the scientist at his home back in Richmond. To this day, Marianne still ribs me for buying her that tawdry crop top souvenir, instead of picking her up some decent Fresno swag that she could have then flaunted in front of all the ladies down at the Richmond Savings Credit Union on No. 3 Road, where she then worked as a perky teller. I often wondered if Marianne was just mad because only a few days earlier I got to swoon over Princess Diana as she passed within inches of me when I was asked as a plainclothes officer to help guard a table of champagne during the intermission of the opera production that had been put on for her and Prince Charles at the Orpheum as a part of Expo 86. I think Marianne was miffed that I kept saying the reason Her Highness had fainted the next day down in False Creek was because the real handsome Prince she'd smiled at the evening before, me, was no now nowhere to be seen.

So then, yes, it happened. It was a constructed reality dream come true. In September of 1987 I was finally transferred to the "E" Division Serious Crime Section. It was essentially a flying squad of crack homicide investigators based at 33rd and Heather in Vancouver who were assigned to respond on a moment's notice to just about every fresh murder case that got called in across British Columbia. When I arrived on station all the old-timers there were still hurting bad over their role in cleaning up the Johnson and Bentley file. It was a case where some prick incel slaughtered a family of six who'd been picking blueberries in the bush up near Kamloops. Knowing that the two preteen daughters had been kept alive for a week, and repeatedly raped, was just too much to take. Others on the team were making a periodic contribution to the Air India bombing investigation down the hall—something with which all those white collar crime dimwits over in federal policing were still struggling. Knowing that justice for those 83 children murdered *en masse* back in 1985 was now in the hands of MBA-educated pretty boys—who'd never once looked up from their newspaper to go investigate a real crime—was even harder for them to take. It was a time when real gangsters like Roderick Schnob, Gordon Pawliw, Rodney Camphaug, Sergey Filonov and Eddie Cheese ruled the underworld out on the west coast—far and away more depraved than today's wannabe tossers known as the Red Scorpions, the Bacon Brothers and the Brothers Keepers. It was a time when *real* criminals with *actual* street creds ended up in Oakalla Prison over in Burnaby where *real* shot callers ordered you to your death at Friday morning prayers if you didn't put in the work—unlike all these modern-age day spas called regional pretrial centres. Over the next four long years I would travel to every nook and cranny of B.C.—usually by Citation jet or twin engine King Air. I was out of town more often than I was at home in Steveston with Marianne. I'm pretty sure Fort Nelson and Powell River were the only two places I never got to visit. When I first arrived on the unit I was assigned to serve on a taskforce that had been pulled together to review 17 cold case murders, including a couple that fell under non-RCMP jurisdiction—in places like Vancouver and Saanich where we Mounties were absolutely detested by all the local detectives. Still stinging from Clifford Olson missteps, RCMP senior management wanted to make sure we didn't have yet another serial killer on the loose in B.C. Through all our collective effort we ended up solving four out of the 17 cases within the first year of operation. One of those cases—involving the arrest and charge of Jean Victor Beaulac for the murder of an Indigenous woman—not only became the very first Mr. Big undercover case in all of Canada, it still stands today as *the* seminal Supreme Court of Canada decision on language rights for accused persons. When I reflect back on the four very intense years I spent there—both on the taskforce and on the fresh murder response go team—it's just so sad how many innocent souls lost their lives to so many savage predators. I'm getting old now, but names like Colleen Shook, Marguerite Telesford, Rachel Turley, Mary Ann Costin, Pauline Johnson, Tracey Chartrand, Crystal Hogg and Linda Tatrai still come to mind for me. Every day as I set about my gardening and my humble chore doing, yet another name and face comes to mind. These were real human beings, not inches of copy in the local daily newspaper. Whether it was the battered body of a drug dealer left abandoned on Wreck Beach, or bits and pieces of human flesh found embedded in explosion debris in the Newhawk Goldmine up near Hyder, Alaska—or the words "Who Am I" carved into the back of the head of 13-year-old Jamie Bains, I got to see it all. It broke my heart 33 years later when several Vancouver radio stations reported that some older kid in Surrey was believed to be the youngest victim of gang violence in B.C. history. I guess Jamie being a member of a violent street gang known for stealing eight cars every day in Vancouver, who ends up being tortured as a suspected police informant for four days in a row with a red-hot clothing iron in some dank East Van closet—then suffocated and tossed from a moving car out near UBC—doesn't really count for much these days. Unlike all those short-memory reporters, I actually had to hold Jamie's hand as he was zipped up in his body bag. I was instrumental in helping to bring to justice his three gang violence killers. It was at a time when there was no such thing as dashcam video or smartphone idiocy, so there was a *real* obligation on the part of homicide detectives to go do *real* policework and talk face-to-face with *real* humans. Somehow I also found the time to throw in on the Pattison-family kidnapping case and help capture two dangerous lifers who'd shot their way out of Kent Prison with M-16 rifles and a hijacked helicopter. Man, what a way to spend my early thirties. While all my coworkers were spending $8 on gasoline, in order to save $4 on milk and cheese down in Blaine, Washington on their days off, I spend all my scarce spare time writing legally airtight wiretap affidavits at the kitchen table—all while bottle feeding baby Megan on my lap.

In the spring of 1991, I was promoted to corporal and transferred to Chilliwack, first as a young supervisor on the plainclothes investigation section at Chilliwack RCMP Detachment, and finally as the guy in charge of the major crime section for the entire upper Fraser Valley. At the local city detachment I quickly got involved in the investigation of bank robberies, sexual assaults, and of course more fresh-case homicides. My first big assignment there was to track down—and extradite back to Canada from the Philippines—a revered court official who had sexually assaulted 6 small children from all across the local community. The case had already been investigated by the time I arrived on station, so my job was strictly to find out where he went after he'd skipped bail. It took a while, but I finally got him. His name was Martin Bakker and he was getting on in age. On the plane back to Canada from Manila in the fall of 1993 my first instincts were to throttle him when nobody was looking, but after 10 hours of listening to the story of what it was like to grow up as a small boy in Dutch Indonesia in the early 1940s, I developed an all new appreciation for who he really was. I learned with great horror that when the Japanese Imperial Army invaded his homeland in 1942, they immediately murdered his father right in front of him and his trembling mother. The two of them only survived the war because they had been taken to a nearby death camp where they were used as sex slaves. His mom was raped up to 20 times per day for three years. He was repeatedly buggered and forced to perform oral sex on drunk soldiers at least twice a day for the duration. It was the only way they could get worm-infested rice and rancid drinking water from their captors. I guess turning into a pedophile was both unforgivable and understandable at the same time. When our flight landed in Honolulu, he was taken away by U.S. Marshalls for two days of interim detainment. I was taken away by taxi to the nearby airport Holiday Inn, which due to its logo and branding prompted a painful trigger event that drew out the unexpected flashback of my own anguished childhood. It caused me to cower in my room and cry constantly before Bakker and I were once again reunited two days later for our final flight back home to Vancouver. Luckily my room in Honolulu was on the ground floor, so I was never really at risk to be held upside down by my ankles. Luckily there was nothing outside my room that even closely resembled the icy Detroit River. When I got home to Chilliwack I was never more happy to caress Marianne and Megan and our newborn, Alena. Everyone wanted to hear all about my trip. After all, it had involved a barnstorm through Hong Kong, Manila and Honolulu in just six days—and a requirement on my part to counter a last-ditch bid by Bakker to evade extradition by forcing me to "out bribe" an airport official on the tarmac to gain clearance for that aging Air Philippines 747 to take off in swelting 46°C heat at midnight. Shit, I just wanted to mow the lawn, take out the trash—and maybe watch a little A&E. I was worried I might not get reimbursed for that $800 "airport exit fee" begrudgingly forked over by me while acquiescent Canadian embassy staffers looked on.

After I moved upstairs to take over daily leadership of that regional major crime section in December of 1992—just four weeks after Alena was born—my first big assignment was to dust off an old cold case that had become the talk of every hotshot homicide investigator across British Columbia for over 16 years. It was a case involving the 1977 shotgun execution murder of 38-year-old Lazlo Mihaly Vegh. Although media reports had been describing him as a career criminal and a drug dealer, a close read of the case file revealed he had actually been a kingpin in the Hungarian mafia and a central player in Vancouver's seedy underworld in the 1970s. He had been one of thousands of violent criminals who'd immigrated to Canada in 1957 following the Hungarian Revolution of 1956. Having murdered about as many Soviet-invasion troops as he had been able to get his hands on, he arrived here afraid of nothing and nobody. He didn't have a scar on his face, but he arrived ready to create mayhem and to do just about anything to get the power. His naked and frozen body had been found by highway maintenance workers stuffed inside a steamer trunk at the bottom of a 100' cliff, just east of Hope toward the end of January 1977. In addition to two close-range shotgun blasts to the torso, the autopsy revealed that the back of his skull had also been bashed in postmortem.

What had made the Vegh murder case so difficult to solve was the fact that his body had been found without any identification, and his fingerprints weren't on file with Headquarters Ottawa. It wasn't until somebody recognized an artist sketch of his face that had been posted in *The Province* newspaper in 1983 that he was finally identified. It was a small break in the case that allowed all the hotshot investigators to focus all their efforts in exactly all the wrong places. Because Vegh had been living around the corner from Gladstone Secondary at the time of his last known sighting on January 4, 1977—in the vicious 'Clark Park Gang' controlled part of town known as East Van—and because he was a high-ranking mobster with a known violent history, it only followed, right, that we tunnel-vision cops should concentrate all our inquiries on seedy biker bars and stripper clubs? What all these hotshot investigators had been seeing for 16 years was a famous gangster who'd unquestionably been the victim of a contract killing. Without such a theory of the case there would have never been any opportunity for everyone to join Mötley Crüe and the Heathens of Howe Street down at the Marble Arch to chat up naked peelers—maybe even hive off the odd, fortuitous blowjob.

What I saw, after just two days of reading through the 11 banker's boxes that formed the basis of the cold case file, was a fucking coward and spousal abuser who deserved to be blasted by a shotgun at close range—and to have his fucking head bashed in postmortem. What I saw were case details that surfaced after the body had been finally identified in 1983 that revealed the fucking prick had been questioned by the Anaheim Police Department in December of 1976 for his role in the violent assault of his common-law wife, Donnaline Caplette. What I saw was another fucking Holiday Inn, and a family on a Christmas vacation to Disneyland, wherein the coward prick husband beats the wife senseless, tearing her ear off to point where it has to be surgically reattached at the nearby ER. What I saw was an autopsy report that showed Vegh's body had been gingerly wrapped in a floral-print quilt that would only ever be purchased by a mother looking for sewing notions and school supplies over at the Hudson's Bay in Park Royal. What I saw were the careful actions of a killer who had gone to great lengths to shroud a body, and make sure it would be dumped as far away as possible from a cowering child and a terrified mom. I liked strippers just as much as the next bonehead Mountie, but I was smart enough to know that the underworld would never dispose of a body like this. Underworld gangsters don't just kill their enemies, they display their corpses on the front steps of Yaletown restaurants so as to send a message to everyone: don't ever fuck with us again. Survivors of family violence don't just kill their abusers in self-defence, they bash their fucking heads in postmortem so as to send an equally blunt message: take that, you miserable fucking prick.

After four days of reading the case file I knew exactly who the killer was. I was absolutely certain it was Donnaline. She had been 28 years old at the time. There was next-to-zero family history detailed in the file, but I was willing to bet the lives of Megan and Alena there had also been incest committed on that 10-year-old daughter who had been living in the family home. The pathology of parent-on-child incest was just something with which I felt weirdly familiar. As I brought forward my theory of the case to my bosses I knew it wasn't going to be easy to pull together a prosecution-ready case. We were still lacking that one last piece of evidence we needed to make an arrest, and the organizational culture of the RCMP at the time was never going to go for a young buck like me being the one who would get all the credit for solving the biggest cold case in the province. After all, I was that guy who always got mocked behind his back for being that autistic savant prick who would always solve big cases; who would always end up in the news for arresting psychiatrists with fancy names like Dr. Tyhurst for historical sex slave allegations dating back to the very beginnings of the CIA. I had just gotten a voluntary confession from Keith Harrison for murdering his 7-year-old stepson out near Hell's Gate, so it was an absolute imperative that I be summarily destroyed. The whole idea of stiffing me with this tricky cold case file was to set me up to catastrophically fail—and shut me the fuck up.

The good news was that directly under my command at the time was the very best major crime investigator in the entire country. His name was Constable Bob Paulson, but I just called him Bobby. I kid you not, he was the very best. Eighteen years later he would go on to become Commissioner of the RCMP, and deservedly so. As a dynamic duo of criminal investigators, he and I were fucking unstoppable. I kid you not, you could put any big case in front us—Jimmy Hoffa, JonBenét Ramsey, Amelia Earhart—and we would have it solved by sundown. He and I pretty much detested each other on a personal level, but there was no denying our true crime fighting chemistry. I only wish he hadn't selected that cringeworthy line from *True Romance* as his default catch phrase. I always went with "nobody listens to Russ Grabb," but constantly pondering "if you had to fuck a guy" really wasn't my cup of tea. Visualizing Bobby in the throes with Johnny Depp just seemed so very wrong. I would have guessed Ethan Hawke for him.

Tapping into Bobby's unequalled genius, we put together a theory that if Donnaline had indeed killed Vegh, she would have had her 10-year-old daughter right there at her side. She would have lured Vegh into the basement after supper on January 4, 1977, on the pretext that the washing machine was on the fritz. Upon his arrival downstairs—all drunk and ready to smack her around—she would have blasted him twice with a preloaded shotgun. Channeling six years of simmering rage, she would have then used the butt end of the shotgun to crush the back of his fucking head. As an SFU grad with high intelligence, she would have known that the basement would to be the spot do the deed because a cement floor would be easier to clean than a living room carpet. As a good person who'd never before killed anyone, she would have fucked up terribly by not realizing that once Vegh's body had been encased in that steamer trunk, there would have been no way she could ever lift it up the stairs and slide it into her pre-waiting Chevy van. She would have to sleep on it overnight, and call a local moving company in the morning to inquire if a couple of bruisers could drop by and load a steamer trunk into a vehicle for a couple hundred bucks under the table.

That was our theory, and it worked brilliantly. We drew up a list of every single moving company that had been in existence in Vancouver in January of 1977, and off Bobby went. Within a matter of days he had not only found the company and the two bruisers who took the job 16 years earlier, one of them took Bobby straight to the murder scene in the 2200 block of East 24th Avenue without any prompting or hints from any external source. It was the missing piece of evidence that we needed to boogie up to Nelson House in northern Manitoba to arrest Donnaline where she was then teaching Indigenous children. We didn't get everything correct with our washing machine scenario, but we were able to confirm that there indeed had been incest and a long history of family violence in the home. Vegh had even once put a loaded gun to Donnaline's face and a sharp sword to her throat. There was no doubt it came down to a matter of killing him, or being killed yourself—leaving your 10-year-old daughter to be raped again by daddy and sex trafficked to a bunch of obese pedophiles over in St. Petersburg, Russia. With her husband working for the mob at the time, calling VPD for help was not an option.

On February 8, 1993, when all the newspapers in B.C. reported that Donnaline Elanora Caplette, age 49, would be appearing in Provincial Court today for the alleged second degree murder of Lazlo Mihaly Vegh in 1977, my landline literally melted off the hook. Every single hotshot homicide investigator from here to Timbuktu called to blast me for yet again having the temerity to solve the unsolvable. Their dastardly plan to see the white sheep of the RCMP family fail miserably had gone horribly south. It took me all of three months to ruin their day on a 16-year-old case. All the ladies down in the steno pool looked at me like I'd just invented fire for Heaven's sake. One even asked if she could have my baby. All the men in the building just looked away and refused to make eye contact. It was all I could do not to go up to the roof and yell, "In your face, mothafuckas!" As much as I was still a recalcitrant little child at heart, I still found a way to keep up the illusion that I was a mature adult. I somehow found a way to bite my tongue and keep the conversation focused on last night's lame episode of *Seinfeld*. Two months later the brass would take another run at me by ordering me to work in uniform at the global summit between Presidents Bill Clinton and Boris Yeltsin in Vancouver. Being assigned to guard a lamppost on the motorcade route for three days in a row was their way of telling me they were still in charge, and I was someone they could still fuck with if I didn't watch my step.

In January of 1995, when prosecutor Greg Weber called me at home one evening to ask whether or not—as the lead case investigator—I would have any issue with Donnaline pleading guilty to manslaughter and receiving zero prison time, I of course said, "Absolutely not, go for it." When she appeared before B.C. Supreme Court Justice Wally Oppal on February 7, 1995, he gave her a 12-month suspended sentence. Unaware that I too had something to do with it, Justice Oppal commended Greg Weber in open court for agreeing to the light sentence. Citing the Supreme Court of Canada decision in *Regina v. Angelique Lavallee* on the battered wife defence, he said, "Society needs no protection from Ms. Caplette. I find it most disturbing that as we approach the 21st century we as a society still have not yet found a cure for this sickness, this sickness of violence against women." The case was soon showcased all across Canada as a good example of where battered women might finally be making justice headway on the whole question of intimate partner violence in the family home.

I had kept my promise to one day solve a really big cold case that would produce noble downstream benefit for society at large. In 2001, when I went before a selection board in order to seek a promotion to superintendent to take over the police sciences school and major crime investigation program at the Canadian Police College in Ottawa, I revealed that over the course of my full RCMP career I had participated to varying degrees in 92 homicide cases. I also slid in the fact that I was the guy chosen to travel to the Prince Albert Penitentiary in 1989 in order to interrogate serial killer Darren Kelly about his involvement in multiple unsolved homicide cases, including the sadistic 1985 murder of 2-year-old Aaron Kaplan in Vancouver. Kelly was serving life in prison for the abduction, rape and murder of 3-year-old Genni May in December of 1985 in Sechelt. It was my way of making the point that I was a suitable candidate to exercise insightful leadership in the field of murder investigations for all police departments across the country. I kept to myself the petulant point that none of my cases had involved the payment of $10,000 per body to secure a conviction. There had only been good old fashioned policework. Shamelessly, I boasted that when the prosecution service in B.C. conducted its quality control screening in the mid-1980s of over 10,000 reports to crown counsel submitted by the police, prosecutor Tom Burns wrote that my submission urging charges of indecent assault against a high school teacher, involving a teenage girl student in Richmond, was far and away the very best and most cleverly articulated submission that he'd ever come across. I did, however, have to apologize to the board for tearing up when I mentioned my modest role in helping to bring to justice the coward who viciously stabbed 27-year-old Donna

Zupancic to death in Burnaby way back in 1982. It was yet another intimate partner violence case that took the life of yet another innocent woman. If I had arrived on scene as a 25-year-old first responder going Code 3 just a couple of seconds earlier she might still be alive today. Skinners who hurt tiny children were already on my imprison-on-sight hit list, but this case prompted me to forever more place dirty wifebeaters squarely in my show-no-mercy crosshairs. When I bumped into Wally Oppal on the streets of Vancouver in the spring of 2021, we kibitzed about the two of us having made real history in this Vegh case. He mentioned all the guff he took for the bullshit assertion from pig men everywhere that his sentencing of Donnaline had made it open season on husbands. I mentioned that I'm sure in my own way I had brought closure for Donnaline and her daughter. He didn't bite. As he sauntered off with his trademark limp, he said, "Be sure to give my very best to Megan. She's without a doubt the top restaurant honcho in the city." So it seems it really was true. Nobody does listen to Russ Grabb. But voices do carry. You see that, right?

# CHAPTER 8: Easy to Be Hard

AS I NOW progress through my sixties I'm starting to realize that reflection—sensible reflection—might just be the path to safety and inner peace I've been searching for all my life. I don't yet have all the answers I need to go to my grave a fully contented man, but I'm starting to sense that I'm very close to something very big. Even with my ongoing battle with incurable leukemia cancer—and all that led up to my brush with death in May of 2020 from neutropenic sepsis and acute kidney failure—I'm certain the missing piece for me can't be very far away. It may well be that writing this memoir will turn out to be the very thing that I needed to do all along in order to figure it all out. As I reflect even further on my rather extraordinary life I'm constantly struck by the nature and number of crazy coincidences that always seem to come my way. It's almost as if the universe has been trying to tell me something—that perhaps there is a destiny for me that lays beyond running from my past and always creating no end of chaos and heartache for those I love. Maybe I really am that flawed romantic who strangely flirts with danger and dysfunction, whose ethos pulls back the curtain on human frailty—and unearths the gritty texture of life and living in a barren world that has no shame and shows no mercy.

When it comes to crazy coincidences we certainly can't discount that creepy tangential connection between me and serial killer Paul Bernardo. I often wonder what kind of predatory life I might have lived had I not made that French Foreign Legion leap to the RCMP. Without the voice of Grandpa Fred in the background, there's little doubt in my mind I too would have ended up in Millhaven or some shit. There was just so much simmering rage and unbearable rejection to channel. It's only now starting to settle down. I suppose it's even more crazy that my eldest sister Vicky had been one of several eager teenagers who were depicted in that iconic Trudeaumania picture of Pierre Elliott Trudeau campaigning at the Malton Airport in 1968. You know, the one that was plastered on the front page of every daily newspaper in Canada. She was the pretty girl standing beside him with that Brownie Hawkeye camera in her hand. I guess it's crazy because it would be her younger brother Russell who would end up meeting 11-year-old Justin on December 31, 1982, while his mother Margaret exchanged creepy-ish kisses with that off-duty RCMP sergeant in the hallway of the Whistler Creek Lodge. This of course doesn't even take into account the fact that it would be her nieces Megan and Alena who would be shown on the local television news in Ottawa on September 30, 2000, kneeling before the flag-draped casket of the former prime minister in Parliament's Centre Block—or that Russell would end up being the French-speaking police spokesperson who would be called upon to go on national television in November of 1998 in order to explain to the Canadian public and a bedridden "northern magus" back in Montreal just how things were progressing following the tragic loss of his son in an avalanche near Nelson. Dare I again mention that my time up there required me to help comfort a then 28-year-old Justin, or that it was the *New York Times* who quoted me most extensively on this file down in the States? I soon received no end of messages from ordinary Quebecers praising me for just how authentically I spoke to their collective grief and shock by addressing them in their language with simple grace and relatable diction.

So while all this jibber-jabber about a serial killer and a future prime minister sounds like pretty shocking stuff, we really need to stay focused here. For me personally the very first crazy coincidence that always seems to come to mind is the fact that January 4, 1977—in other words, the very day that Donnaline killed Lazlo Vegh in preemptive self-defence—is the exact date when I popped that what-was-I-thinking letter in the mail to my mother. It was a letter that would cement my fate for at least 42 more years, and make it next to impossible for me to convince my siblings that what their mother had done to me when I was young—while their father turned a blind eye—did indeed happen as I now describe it in excruciating detail. It was quite a letter, and its content and an analysis as to why I wrote it now seems to be the very question upon which I must focus. As I always say to those who ask, it's not sudden death that I fear the most: it's the suffering that comes with leukemia. It's the reality that I may soon die without ever having figured out what I really needed to know in order to go in peace. As I say, writing this memoir and thinking through all the machinations of my life—and how they all weave together with such elaborate truth-exposing intricacy— may just be the path to getting it right before it's too late. I'm not a doomsday kinda guy, but I can read a lab report. I know what having next to no lymphocytes in my bone marrow—right in the middle of a pandemic—really means. I have a pretty good idea what the word "incurable" seeks to convey. Thinking through and laying bear that fateful 1977 letter might just be my very own Amelia Earhart discovery moment.

It all started in the summer of 1976. I was 19. I had just graduated from high school. My parents and my three younger brothers—two still in high school and one still in grade school— had all packed up and moved from Scarborough to Tillsonburg to find greener pastures. My two older sisters—one majoring in history, the other studying to become a nurse—were off doing their thing at the University of Toronto. I was still hoping to get a call up to the RCMP based on my application submitted in Grade 11, but my immediate plan was to follow through with my acceptance to the architectural sciences program at Ryerson. The Province of Ontario still had Grade 13 in those days, so I was fast approaching my twenties by the time I was finally free to pursue post-secondary education, and go chase an exciting career out in the real world. If I didn't soon get that call from the RCMP, I swore I was going to become the next great Arthur Erickson architect of Canada. There would be no stopping me, right?

So before heading off to find a decent roommate for university, there was first that little matter of the 1976 Summer Olympics in Montreal. That's right, all through high school I had worked part time at several different McDonald's restaurants across Scarborough. By Grade 13 the company had taken the unusual step of promoting me to assistant manager even though I was just a kid with a 10-speed bicycle—who was only ever free to work in the evenings and on weekends. Despite my protests to the contrary, they just kept telling me that I was unusually gifted in modern business operations and leadership. With what was expected to be the busiest McDonald's on the planet soon to open at Atwater Avenue and Sainte-Catherine in downtown Montreal, they were in dire need of good people to head up there right away, and man the fort for the duration of the games. I didn't speak a damn word of French back then, but it was sure enough one hell of a fun time—and a great learning experience. Billeted in some fancy hotel, it was the sexually charged place where I finally lost my virginity. I had been very popular with the ladies back in high school, but after what I had endured as a young child the very last thing I ever wanted to see after Grade 6 was yet another vagina with hair. As it turns out, there were plenty of *jolies femmes* up there willing to help me overcome my hesitations.

After coming home from Montreal, I ended up sharing an apartment just off Spadina and Bloor in downtown Toronto with my best friend Noel Windfeld from high school. He was enrolled in the engineering program at U of T, so it only made sense that two pocket-protector mathletes with limited funds should end up bunking in together. I say limited funds because although I had saved up the modern-age equivalent of $80,000 while working at McDonald's, I knew my whole five-year degree program was going to cost me at least $300,000 in books, tuition, art supplies and living expenses. Unlike my two older sisters, I had been a few high-school GPA points short of scholarship qualification, and with no parents to rely on I knew this was going to be a tough nut to crack. I was really hoping the RCMP would call soon so I could start raking in that super stellar starting salary of $12,500 per year. I say mathlete because in high school I had been a whiz at calculus, algebra, relations and functions, physics, chemistry and oh ya, English composition. It had just made so much sense to cower behind the armour of all those immutable equations and unassailable poetic truths, rather than confront the lonely and troubled Janis Ian face that I saw every morning in the mirror—especially at 17.

So, by the end of December 1976—pretty much around the same time that Lazlo Vegh was tearing Donnaline's ear off at that hotel near Disneyland—I was quite stoked that I was rocking the grades at Ryerson. On the other hand, I was most perplexed by the fact that I was being overtaken by this suffocating malaise that I just couldn't shake. I had every good reason to celebrate the long-awaited escape from my childhood, and to wallow in all the good fortune I was currently enjoying while living on my own with my best buddy from high school. All those wild nights drinking beer at the El Mocambo tavern down the street were just so much fun. So many live bands to enjoy. So many random celebrities coming in and out. There was even word the Rolling Stones were scoping the place out to record their latest album. But no matter how hard I tried, I just kept getting dragged down by this gripping sense of impending doom. The feelings of shame and despair were becoming simply unbearable. There were days when—for no good reason—I just felt like smashing every stick of furniture in our apartment. There were nights when I used calculus to map out the speed at which I needed to be running in order to jump with absolute suicidal precision in front of a subway at the Dundas station near campus. It was so hard to hold on. I just wanted to die. I should have never had sex with that Véronique girl up in Montreal. It was a terrible mistake. What was I thinking? Sex was the very thing that almost got me killed in 1965. Sex was the thing that robbed me of my childhood. Avoiding sex at all costs had always been my way of coping back in high school. If it hadn't been for that older kid, Terry Mercury—and all his fatherly advice in the gym and out on the football pitch after school—I would have been dead before Grade 11. Terry had unknowingly saved me from all those non-stop suicidal ruminations. But now something had to be done. Something had to happen real quick, or else I would never make it to my 20$^{th}$ birthday coming up in just four months. The sadness was overwhelming. Thoughts of suicide were growing even more intense.

So let's just hit pause for one second. Ask anyone in my shoes what's the absolute worst thing you could ever ask a survivor of childhood violence and sexual defilement, no matter how severe or minor it really was? Ask us and we'll tell you straight up that it's the very thing you tone-deaf Canadians always ask. You just can't help yourself, can you? You always ask, "Why didn't you say anything at the time? Why didn't you fight back? Why didn't you run away? Why did it take you 60 years to come forward?" When it comes to female survivors, your very first inclination is to ask, "What were you wearing?" I say absolute worst because being presented with these types of questions—after what we've just been through—is akin to being raped yet again. They all come trigger loaded with the inference that maybe we're fabricating everything. You're putting the onus on the pedestrian innocently walking along the sidewalk to prove that the truck that just mowed them down actually drove off the road—and that it wasn't them who inflicted hideous injuries upon themselves in order to get their name in the paper.

What you Canadians always fail to understand is that these predators not only have zero concern for the lives of the innocent humans upon which they prey, they more than any other cohort in our miserable species instinctively understand that what motivates us all more than anything else—and thus what keeps us all eternally captive to some external master—is our insatiable need to belong, to matter, and to be loved for who we really are. Once a demented mother has that hook in her prey, she can get away with just about anything. Once an abusive husband holds that alluring power over his wife, there's really no end to what she'll let him do to her. Whether it's a small child or an adult woman, we all eventually come to equate physical pain and imposed misery with affectionate love. After a while, we just can't tell the difference.

What you Canadians always fail to understand is that even after we survivors are ready to make a break for it, the shame that we feel for our own actions is simply too much to bear. We'll do anything to avoid talking about it. What sane woman is ever going to admit that she allowed her spouse to repeatedly beat her because his supper was cold? What 7-year-old boy from Bramalea is ever going to admit to his friends at school that he performs cunniligus on his mother down the street at 30 Brentwood Drive? Just ask Sheldon Kennedy why he wrote a memoir titled, *Why I Didn't Say Anything.* All that shame leads to crushing despair, and all that crushing despair leads to thoughts of suicide and urgent self-destruction through drugs, alcohol—and in the case of dumbass mathletes like me—unbridled erotic exploration with feral cat females whose physical appearance and underlying pathology feel strangely familiar.

Of all the hundreds of people who I would count as a close friend, only one of you have ever asked, "Oh my God, Russ. You poor bastard. How did you ever survive? Is there anything I can do?" The rest of you simply corrected my verb tenses and lectured me on how to write a book with industry standard perfection—in other words, how to turn immutable poetic truths into Netflix-friendly tripe. Only one of you ever really wanted to understand how it was that I was able to navigate such madness at such a young age. But anyway, enough about Marianne. The answer to this question goes back to what I once said about compartmentalization: when you're too small to fight and too young to flee, you simply reconfigure reality inside your brain. Some children for example conjure up imaginary friends with whom they share all their fears. It's what Andy meant by 'second cousin to Harvey the Rabbit' in *Shawshank Redemption*. For the rest of us mere mortals, well, we simply blame ourselves and idolize our tormentors. It's a quick and easy way to survive the unsurvivable. After all, if our tormentors are perfect beings with absolutely no faults, then it only follows that they could never have done anything bad to us. It actually follows that nothing bad ever happened, period. We just will it so in our brains.

On January 4, 1977—the very day that poor Donnaline had no choice but to kill or be killed—I too needed a preemptive strike. If I didn't do something quick, I was going to toss myself in front of a subway at exactly 7:38 a.m. the next morning. Mathematical calculations had confirmed it was the optimal time and location to cobble together the maximin number of eyewitnesses to my suicide. Hundreds of people would gasp at the sight of my horrific death. What better way to say I mattered, and was loved on some horribly cruel level. I knew exactly what I had to do. Despite everything that happened to me as a young child, I would sit down at the kitchen table and write the most loving and complimentary letter to my mom that I could possibly ever write. I would tell her what a great person she had been, and thank her profusely for all that she did for me during such trying economic times. By the time I was finished, she would be portrayed as a living Saint. It would follow that she had no faults whatsoever. It would follow that she could have never done anything bad to me. It would mean relief from crushing despair. It would mean tunneling deep inside my brain would be exactly how I would manifest my primordial instinct to fight or flight. I knew I better get a move on. I had a fateful letter to pop in the mail before thermodynamics class down at the quad today at noon. I also had a book report to do on Margaret Atwood's new novel, *Surfacing*. I had been told it was a cautionary tale about a young protagonist whose quest for clarity goes horribly sideways after a troubled visit to Quebec one random summer. Not the summer of 1976, but random. Oh come on, what sensible person is ever going to believe such shit? I have hundreds of close friends who couldn't give a flying fuck either way. How about you? Are ready to hear what it's really like to survive the unsurvivable, and to have everybody you know stare at you like you're some pathological liar? As the rock band Three Dog Night would say, "Especially people who care about strangers, who care about evil and social injustice?" So easy to be hard, isn't it? You see that now, right?

# CHAPTER 9: Simply Celestial

ONE YEAR AFTER Bob Paulson and I cracked the Vegh murder case, I was transferred to Ottawa for two years in order to participate in what was then known as the Headquarters Familiarization Program. It was an offshoot of the High Potential Development Program that had been set up by the RCMP in the 1980s to groom young talent who they thought might one day become Commissioner. I stayed in the program until I was transferred back to B.C. in 1996 where my three big taskings— before becoming the lead media spokesperson in 1997—were to firstly find out which VPD detective at CLEU was leaking intel to local Asian-based organized crime, secondly, interview a local television reporter as a murder suspect on behalf of the Nova Scotia RCMP, and finally, help launch a joint FBI-RCMP taskforce that would very soon take down a violent organized crime consortium operating out of Boston. I'm talking about a nasty gang of thugs that was trafficking heroin down there and planning a contract killing up here. Back on the Headquarters Familiarization Program, I had been one of 20 supervisors plucked from the ranks from all across the country to participate. Ever the systemically racist and misogynistic outfit, there wasn't a single woman or person of colour in the mix. It was the beginning of the end for this globally revered organization. All it would take was the arrival of some narcissist from Italy and the Force would be in a downward spiral of organizational atrophy from which it would never recover. That prick actually became Commissioner on September 2, 2000. The rest is history. Painful history. When Bobby became Commissioner in 2011 he did his very best as a former jet pilot instructor with the Air Force to pull the nose up, but it was ostensibly too late. To this day, I'm still saddened that the very guy who did what he could to right the ship is the one still taking all the heat. What my buddy Justin never really understands is that when it comes to selecting the right person to serve as RCMP Commissioner, or even astronauts who want to become Governor General, 'best in show' is still a dog. Do your homework, Pumpkin. Celebrities always make for real shitty leaders.

Anyway, while I was stationed in Ottawa on this occasion I got to work with a group of Indigenous Inuit people and some academics from SFU on the design of the revolutionary new policing model for the Eastern Arctic in anticipation of the new Canadian Territory of Nunavut coming online in 1999. Because I had a strong background in homicide investigations, I was soon asked to co-author the Green Paper that led to the White Paper that was used to enact Bill C-104 in Parliament. It allowed for the creation of the National DNA Data Bank of Canada. It was pretty cool being the guy who ghost wrote the Minister's response to the 1994 Oppal Report on policing in B.C., but it was most painful having to craft words with which I could not agree. I thought what Wally had to say about slowly phasing out the RCMP made total sense. I was also once called into the office of Commissioner Phil Murray to receive his praise for my work on the new community policing model for the RCMP in those provinces and territories where the Force does real policework, as opposed to that lame federal law enforcement stuff over in Ontario and Quebec. But the best part of this two-year executive development tour of Headquarters Ottawa was a 9-month program of French immersion over in Gatineau. During the language aptitude screening process, I was summarily called into the office of the woman in charge of candidate selection down at Public Service Canada. She said I was being denied entry because according to my tone recognition and my word enunciation evaluations there was no way in hell I was ever going to become bilingual with any amount of classroom or one-on-one training. After a long chat, she finally relented. She said, "Alright Mr. Grabb. I see here that your memory retention scores are simply off the charts. It seems your memory retention is at the 98 percentile. I used to administer the Stanford-Binet and track the Flynn Effect when I was in post-grad at McMaster, so I know from experience that this means you're probably at or near Mensa-IQ. I'm starting to think you might just be one of those candidates who succeed not because of some innate ability to learn a new language, but because of your rare ability to memorize and play back in your mind the underlying syntax and enabling diction. What'd you think, Mr. Grabb? Shall we go ahead with this?"

Well no kidding we went ahead with this. Well for sure I passed with flying colours. Well of course I became fluent in French in just six months. Despite all my protests to the contrary for three decades, it was indeed because I had memorized everything. Even now I don't actually speak French from the heart, or with natural ease. When engaged in a French conversation, I follow the lead of Russell Crowe in *A Beautiful Mind*, and project the words up on the picture screen in my brain, and move them around until I get it right. I do this at the speed of light so you'd never know I was struggling to find my next meaningful sentence. I tell you all this not because I want to brag about some look-at-me talent that I have. I tell you all this so you will believe me without question when I say that I recall every single word of the conversation that took place between my mother and two female neighbours at 2:17 p.m. on December 28, 1960. We were in the kitchen of our family bungalow, then situated at 10 Brampton Road, Etobicoke. I was 3 years old. I was sitting on the lap of one of two neighbours as she went on and on about how handsome I was—and how much I resembled that famous wrestler, Gorgeous George. I tell you all this so you will have zero doubt in your mind that as the three of them passed me around like some adorable little puppy— and spoke incessantly about Hurricane Hazel of 1954 and the upcoming inauguration of Jack Kennedy in January of 1961—it was indeed true that they each took their turn pulling down my pants and remarking at just how cute my tiny little penis was. Each took a turn fondling and trying to make erect my penis as if I were some sort of amusing novelty. When I say each, I include my very own mother. The subtext of everything was that because I was so adorably handsome, it wasn't really their fault. It was to be expected, right? They had no idea—nor did they even care—that I was mortified with embarrassment. I repeatedly told them to stop, but they simply dismissed me as being cranky, and very much in need of a nap. It amounted to the kind of perverse logic that was employed when that famous male feminist simply dismissed a female reporter as being cranky and on her period when she objected to his slimy hand being placed on her ass at some bar in Creston. It was the beginning of the end for me. I had nothing but pleasant memories of everything up to this point, but from this moment onward it would be Russell George Grabb—actually little Gorgeous George—who would be in a downward 2G spiral from which he might never recover. It would take a kindly earth angel from Peterborough and multiple brushes with death over 60 years to finally pull the nose up—and prepare this poor fucking bastard for a soft landing over on the other side.

I love my five siblings. I love them very much. Outside of Marianne and the girls, I would count them among the finest human beings I've ever met in my life. Lord knows they probably have their own heart-wrenching stories to tell. Lord knows, they've probably seen it all too. As a brother, I couldn't be any more proud of who they are, and how they've lived their lives. But what they all never really understood—and couldn't possibly ever know because I wrote that stupid fucking letter to their mother in 1977—was that some very, very bad things did indeed happen to me back when I was quite young. I'm not a pathological liar. I'm not spinning some elaborate yarn in order to get my name in the paper. I was hurt very badly and I cried so many tears. It's any wonder I'm still alive today to talk about it. Lord knows almost nobody I know could give a shit in any event—at least not those humans who claim to be my close friend.

And because I had remained largely distant from my five siblings as an adult, they also never knew that when I finally retired from the workforce in 2019—after 42 years of going full tilt in every different direction—I was at the top of my game as a go-to business consultant. It was a little known fact that for 13 years after my retirement from the RCMP in 2006 I had been the owner of a much respected executive advisory firm that went by the name, Russ Grabb & Associates Inc. It was the rebranding of my first company, Better Outcomes Consulting Inc. Although we were a small team, we did really well competing head to head with the likes of IBM, Deloitte, KPMG and Price Waterhouse. Before formal dissolution in 2019, my top private sector clients included: the Fortune 500 firm known as National Instruments of Austin, Texas; a multi-national digital marketing firm based out of Don Mills; and a medium-sized digital-tech conglomeration located in Vancouver. Our job was to work directly with overstressed C-suite executives in the boardroom in order to help them set strategic direction and grow market share. As you would have seen in all our Helijet magazine ad copy, our tagline was *Our Vision is Your Success.* It was a cute little double entendre that certainly did the trick. I wasn't riding off into the sunset as a flashy and flamboyant oil baron with a penchant for attracting police and media attention, but we had been quite successful at everything we'd set out to accomplish. It was my $14,000 per year executive coach who said it was pretty cool being selected for that Don Mills gig based on a referral from the gang down at Point-B Consulting and Silicon Valley.

As I wound down my operations in 2018, my top public sector gigs included: working directly with the Auditor General of B.C. and her senior executive team on finding ways to excel even further at how they collectively steward over the $52 billion annual budget operations of the B.C. Government; working directly with an assistant deputy minister leader on crafting a 5-year strategic action plan for what was then known as the Hospital, Diagnostics and Clinical Services Division of B.C.'s Ministry of Health; and working directly with the Deputy Minister of Finance for the Yukon Government on the design of a new computer system to simplify the annual budgetary process of the Yukon Legislature. Among other things, my work in the Yukon also involved sitting down in a boardroom with 15 deputy ministers to hammer out spending priorities for IT in alignment with the expectations of the math teacher who had just become Premier. I am most proud to say that when the 2017 General Election in B.C. ended with a near virtual tie—and when Elections BC was thrown into a tizzy over a possible snap election and a referendum on proportional representation—it was me who the Chief Elections Officer hired to come in to provide trusted advice on how best to get out of the cul-de-sac and back onto the freeway. My very last engagement before turning off the lights and heading out the door was to copy edit many of the documents that B.C.'s Ministry of Environment and Climate Change Strategy had been crafting in order to win public support for its opposition to the controversial Trans Mountain Pipeline. All of this was primarily made possible by my gutsy decision to move over to Victoria from Coal Harbour in the summer of 2012. It placed me closer to the action. Holding court daily at table 82 at the Cactus Club on Douglas Street kept the sales funnel full. It's where weary government executives went to spill all their state secrets—and shop around for consultants with a half a brain who didn't shill for firms like IBM and McKinsey. And while my competition was down at the Union Club licking the boots of deputy ministers who never wanted their smarmy fingerprints anywhere near the crime scenes of professional service and capital asset procurement, I was up here quietly winning over executive director fall guy buyers with sensible adult conversation about enabling better outcomes for those who actually matter.

I'd certainly come a very long way from flipping burgers, studying architecture, solving murders, designing police service models, waxing poetic with the national media, training the world on use of modern major case management, and cracking down on criminal malfeasance across the upper chain of command of the Canadian Armed Forces. Again, most folks said it was akin to going from Walmart greeter to NASA astronaut. Nobody thought it could be done. But then again, nobody ever listens to Russ Grabb. His own siblings thought he was out west writing traffic tickets and giving kindergarten classes tours of the police station. Surely Russell wouldn't be working on a murder-murder? What would he ever know about that? It was like Whoopi Goldberg dismissively saying Roman Polanski wasn't really guilty of rape-rape. By the time full retirement finally rolled around I was exhausted and ready for that nap those three repugnant sex offenders tried to impose upon me back in December of 1960. So whether it was a 13-year girl being drugged and defiled by some Hollywood fuck back in the 1970s, or my own lifetime of marginalization, I was tired of hearing that observable reality wasn't reality-reality.

So as you can see, I left the workforce with quiet grace in April of 2019. But unlike most folks, there was no gold watch, no going away speech from Joanne over in accounting, and no pitcher of bellinis down at the Tap & Barrel. I just quietly walked away with my RCMP pension thinking what the fuck was that? Who was I, and how did I ever survive such madness? Rather than booking some lame cruise to Alaska, I just wanted to be left alone to think, to reflect upon what all this meant. Unaware I would soon be experiencing the slow early onset symptoms of incurable leukemia—but nonetheless feeling tired and somewhat lost—I soon found myself in mental health therapy at a reputable counseling service over in North Vancouver. It was one of the best things I could have ever done. It was my turn to heal. It was my turn to find peace. Surely to God the day would soon come when I would no longer have to wake up at 3:10 a.m. to scan the room for danger. Surely to God at age 62 it was finally time to put those fast-escape running shoes away for good in the front hall closet.

I was so glad that I'd forced myself into therapy because within a very short period of time I'd told my entire life story to an outstanding clinician who really knew her stuff. She was simply amazing. A true Godsent. For various reasons related to privacy, I've assigned her the safe pseudonym, Dr. Reilly Hagen. After three or four sessions—and after hearing her say nothing but "how did that make you feel" at least seven hundred times—she finally got down to brass tacks. She finally got around to saying, "Alright, Russ. This is good. We're making real progress. What I hear in all your disclosures are two things that really stand out for me. Firstly, I notice that when you're under stress you refer to people as humans or human beings. When you're relaxed or talking about someone or some group for whom you have great fondness—like Indigenous peoples for example—you refer to them as folks, or chaps, or ladies and such. It betrays that you're still very angry at what your mother did to you when you were young. It betrays your strategy to dehumanize the people you detest, ironically by calling them humans. It betrays your belief that we're all part of some cutthroat species of mammals that's completely unable to show compassion for others. You see humans as social cannibals. You have particular disdain for Canadians. I still hear a lot of simmering rage in there. I'm thinking rejection might just be a theme upon which we should focus going forward. Am I correct, Russ?"

After I nodded yes—and tried not to break out into tears—Dr. Hagen continued with, "Alright, next—and most importantly—I see a pattern here. I see an 8 year old boy who thinks it's his sole responsibility to be *the* protector of everyone on the planet, and to save humanity from itself. Isn't that why you solved murders, and put pedophiles in jail, and took on so many consulting contracts in the justice, education and healthcare sectors—turning down so many well-paid contracts with the private sector in the process? To hear you tell it, it seems you gave up your dream to own a house in Whistler so people you didn't even know could have a better life out there. I also see a wounded boy who defines events and moments in time with laboured hyperbole. You say things like, 'it was the moment in human history when' or 'this would be the exact geographic location where.' The pattern tells me that you think what's ailing you—and why it's your job to fix all that's broken across the universe—relates to specific events and milestones that happened when you were young. Are you finally now ready to spill, Russ? Are you ready to stop blaming yourself and idolizing your mother? You didn't break the universe, Russ. Go ahead and cry. It's okay. We'll make a safe place for you here. You're a good person. You're a good man. You did good. Let's pause here for now. Let's reconvene Tuesday at ten."

There was just something in what Dr. Hagen had to say that really with stuck me. There were moments after I got home when I thought I might just be back at that chapel at St. Paul's, begging God to please don't let my special little peanut, Alena, die. I cried non-stop for days. Not only did it make sense to now focus on unearthing specific events and milestones from my childhood, it also felt good to know that I was finally in a safe place where I too might feel like I matter, like I belong, and that someone other than Marianne and the girls might love me for who I really was as a person. Maybe there would even come a day when my five siblings might see me as something other than that crossing guard with an orange vest and a whistle, spinning no end of bullshit about their mom. Maybe one day humans might finally listen to Russ Grabb. Lord knows after surviving two murders attempts, the near death of my very own daughter, and that massive stroke and a calamitous fall in front of that speeding BMW back in 2017, it was pretty much my turn to find my way back home, safe, before the streetlights came on.

Unaware I would soon have to confront the greatest agony of my entire life with cancer, I naively thought that maybe all those people for whom I'd done so much good would finally stop referring to me as that autistic savant prick—and show me a little respect over here. It would take six more weeks of therapy for me to learn that although the branding imposed upon me by my siblings was simply an extension of the maternal narrative that had been cooked up to suffocate anything that might expose an awkward Grabb family truth, Dr. Hagen did indeed have a point: the only way for me to stop being seen as *the* designated crossing guard for the entire celestial universe was for me to simply stop acting like one. The only way for me to stop becoming entangled in a constant stream of chaos and dysfunction was for me to stop thinking I was solely to blame for a broken world. It was time to let go. It was time to forgive myself. It was time to find a way to move forward in my retirement as the good man I'd been all along. It was time to stop doing the impossible for the ungrateful. What would happen next would be very intense. Very intense indeed. It would be analogous to performing open heart surgery on yourself without anesthetics. It would mean having to speak aloud about those things that no small child should ever have to divulge—or live through. But it would be just what I needed to do in order to heal, to find closure, and to undo all the crazy damage I had caused to myself by popping that what-was-I-thinking letter in the mail to my mother way back in 1977.

# CHAPTER 10: The Quiet Revolution

ON MY WAY BACK to see Dr. Hagen on that fateful Tuesday I had a really bad case of butterflies in my stomach. I just knew this was going to be a real gut punch of a therapy session. It kinda reminded me of the nervous anticipation I felt 36 years earlier in Whistler when I was dispatched to the scene of that triple fatal car accident on the highway just south of town. I had been the acting sergeant in charge of Whistler Detachment that week, so it was unavoidable that I had to be the one to go and oversee all the collision reconstruction work being conducted by the Squamish Highway Patrol—and to deal with the coroner. It was that case where three teenaged boys had been driving down to the city from Pemberton in the middle of the night when one of the boys fell asleep at the wheel, plunging their 1970s Ford pickup off a rocky cliff. None of them had been wearing a seatbelt. All three died instantly when they were catapulted through the windshield after their vehicle hit an outcrop of rock on the way down to the bottom of that craggy ravine. Their bodies and body parts were strewn everywhere. One poor young fella had been flung so high into the air, and had landed so hard on his two feet that both his knees had collapsed upwards towards his torso—the exact opposite way our knees are intended to be bent. I had seen it all in my life, but his was far and away the most graphic violation of human flesh I had ever been forced to look at. What had made it so nerve-racking was the fact that on my way down to the scene in my cruiser I already knew what I was about to encounter. The attending officers had already given me the heads up on the police radio to bring an iron stomach. Forcing myself to keep going while imaging the impending horror I was about to see took every ounce of strength I was able to muster. But I just had to go. I had no choice. No choice at all. I was boss man that day. I was in temporarily charge. Everybody was depending on me. It's hard to believe it was 1983. It's hard to believe I was only 26 years old at the time.

So here I was again in 2019. More gut-wrenching reconstruction work to be done. More eviscerated innards strewn everywhere. More heading over somewhere, knowing full well what graphic horror laid in store for me. It took every ounce of strength I was able to muster to open the front door of that mental health services clinic over on the north shore, and to tell Ericka I was here to see Reilly. But I just had to go. I had no choice. No choice at all. My entire future laid in my own hands. It would be up to me to get well. I had but one chance to get this right. I was in essence my own case officer, my own surgeon, my own coroner. Finally, I was in charge of my own destiny. It's hard to believe I was 62 years old, still searching for that iron stomach.

After I got all settled in with Reilly in her office—and after I got over the fact that none of the books on her shelf had been sorted with alphabetical precision—she asked me to finish telling her what I had started to say two weeks ago about Etobicoke and the events of December 28, 1960. She pressed me to explain why I was so bloody certain about the date that those two neighbours had come over to visit my mother. I told her I specifically remembered it was two to three days after Christmas. I specifically remembered I was 3, so it had to be 1960. I told her that I knew this because all my toys from Santa were there in the kitchen, and because all their celebrating over the holidays was pretty much the only thing the three of them had talked about that afternoon. I went on to say that—eventually—they all got around to talking about: the 81 Torontonians who had died from Hurricane Hazel six years earlier; just how handsome Jack Kennedy was, and how they'd all fuck him in a heartbeat if they ever had the chance; and how, according to the local radio news station, today was forecast to be the coldest day on record for Metropolitan Toronto. Finally, I confessed I had nailed down the exact date a couple of months earlier after I randomly came across a CBC news article posted on the internet that said December 28, 2017, was the date when

Toronto had broken its all-time cold temperature record; a record that had been set exactly 57 years earlier on December 28, 1960. I told her that if she didn't believe me she could search engine the phrase, "Extreme cold in Toronto smashes 57-year-old temperature record." She said she trusted every word I had been saying all along, and there was no need for her to fact check me. Like I said, a true Godsent. Finally, somebody other than Marianne and the girls was listening to me. Finally, somebody else seemed to care. I was scared shitless of what I would soon have to disclose, but I was comforted that I was in good hands now with Reilly. I was however worried that I might overwhelm her with all the visceral fury I was about to unleash with scalding hot intensity. When I say "on that fateful Tuesday" I mean what I would end up sharing with Reilly that afternoon would amount to a tumultuous carpet bombing of stinging venom the likes of which she'd probably never before seen. I hoped to God she was ready. It was about to get rabid-animal ugly. You'll forgive me if some of this wretched vitriol soaks through onto these very pages. I did once warn you to brace for impact. I did once say something about a bigger boat.

So ya, merging everything I remembered with precision about Etobicoke—together with that weather fluff piece from CBC—was indeed exactly how I came to discover the exact date when I was first molested as a toddler. It's just how my brain works. Once tasked with a mission to solve a troubling puzzle I almost never give up. Most often it's a matter of personal survival to do so. But there was another reason how I knew December 28, 1960, had been the coldest day in the history of what was then called Metropolitan Toronto, back before it simply became known as the amalgamated City of Toronto. Right after those two nauseating penis fondlers went home—pretty close to supper time—my mother suddenly flew into this absolutely over-the-top fit of burning rage. She even accused me of ruining her big debutante moment. She yelled, "How dare you. How fucking dare you. I go to all this trouble to show off my new hairdo and my brandnew dress, and this is how you repay me? You sit there silent with that God damn Gorgeous George face, acting all puppy dog innocent and stuff, stealing away all the attention. I'm your mother. How could you do such a thing?" Before I could utter a single word, she beat me senseless right on the spot. She'd of course already made sure that my two older sisters were off somewhere else. Trying my level best as a 3-year-old to show that I was a good boy, I remained totally silent. This infuriated her even more. She beat me senseless again. And when I say beat, I don't mean spank. I mean punch and slap. This time I went catatonic. I couldn't believe that my very own mother—the one person who I loved more than anything else in the world, who had always been so loving and kind to me—would do such a thing. So guess what? My catatonic silence infuriated her even more. It denied her the chance to watch me openly suffer. She went to the front hall closet. She grabbed that leather infant walking leash that she had used on me the previous summer. She tore off all my clothes except for my underpants and my ankle socks. She dragged me out to the snowy backyard by my sandy brown hair. She abruptly chained me to the backyard fence and calmy went back inside the house.

Looking back now with my never-quit detective mind, I would guess I had been left out there for no more than 18 minutes, but for me—as a nearly naked 3-year-old—it felt like an eternity. It was -19°C. With the windchill factor it felt like -28°C. It was already starting to get dark. The snow came right up to my knees. The tears streaming down my face froze like sharp icicles, cutting deep into my flesh. When my father came home from work—and as we all sat down for supper as a loving family—he demanded to know why his son Russell had God damn frostbite on his cheeks. My mother joked that I had gone outside to play without permission, without my scarf. This prompted my father to beat me senseless right on the spot and to smash to pieces my favourite toy from Santa: a little wooden doggie on wheels that made an adorable little barking sound when I pulled it along by its string. I was in pain from all the beatings—and of course from the frostbite—but it was the loss of my little Christmas doggie Frankie that hurt the most. It absolutely broke my heart. Rattled to the core, I wet the bed that night. It was a capital crime of childhood recalcitrance for which I would pay with yet another beating from my then 28-year-old mother the very next morning. Fucking cunt. Fucking animal. Bitch.

So ya, at no time did anyone take me to the hospital to have my frostbite checked out. It eventually healed up on its own with the abrasive application of some Nivea cream. This was after all sentimental Canada in 1960. Modern medicine consisted of polio vaccines, iodine, and hot water bottles. Soon pregnant women swooning over American icons like John F. Kennedy, Rock Hudson and Burt Lancaster would be given thalidomide pills to curb morning sickness, completely unaware, and frankly completely unconcerned that by doing so hundreds of babies would soon be born without any arms or legs. This was just how it was in Canada back then. Deformed children—cripples as they were then called—could be handed over to churches for adoption, but morning sickness, well, that was simply unacceptable. There was no concern for the afflicted and the vulnerable. There was a perverse obsession with all things American. As far as it concerned me personally, this was just idyllic Etobicoke. I lived with my loving family at 10 Brampton Road in the heavenly Martingrove neighbourhood. You couldn't pick a more blissful and inviting place to grow up. The closest thing to it would be the setting laid out with poetic precision in the classic film, *Pleasantville*. Not far away lived the Ford family. In a few more years they would give birth to a son who would one day grow up to be Premier of Ontario, but not before allegations would fly about that he dealt hashish in his teens. Even closer would one day live the grandson of the former

Premier of Saskatchewan. He would one day grow up to be one of the most venerated actors in all of Hollywood, but not before he was arrested for criminal assault and possession of a loaded handgun. But enough about Doug Ford and Kiefer Sutherland. Behind everything idyllic, blissful and heavenly back then lurked dark ugly truth, rank hypocrisy, and pious indifference to the suffering of others. Words like venerated, revered and iconic were your first clues as to who were the real criminals out there. If you look closely, you'll see that not much has changed today. Stephen Colbert is going to have to get some new material. We Canadians are anything but polite and apologetic. That's just a branding we've cooked up to disguise who we really are. It germinated in the '50s. It was perfected in the '60s by we sanctimonious boomers. What better way to take without ever having to give back, right? What better way to stealthfully weasel our way into the American psyche? What better way to pretend we know nothing about the 20,000 Indigenous children who we rounded up like cattle in the 1960s—and sent off to sex slave camps masquerading as acclaimed residential schools. Heck, there would even come a day when the Premier of Manitoba and a leading candidate for prime minister in 2021 would both argue that such crimes were all committed in the name of incontestable education and building community. True story. You just can't make this shit up.

As I soon told Reilly, our family moved from Etobicoke to Drummondville, Quebec in the summer of 1961. It was so my father could further his career as a chemical engineer. The child of squalid Russian-immigrant poverty during the Great Depression and World War II, this was his first big break in life. Then in his early thirties, he had been sent there to be the plant manager of a factory that made car batteries for the automotive industry. As the only unilingual anglophone family in town—and with my dad being the boss of so many unionized francophone workers—we weren't very popular. You see, this was the beginning of the Quiet Revolution. It was a turbulent chapter in Canada's history that's never taught in school because it doesn't involve European fur traders handing out Starbucks gift cards and Blue Jays tickets to enslaved Indigenous peoples, or sexy anecdotes about what all those super-cool Americans were doing down south. You see, what the pious Rideau Club culture in Upper Canada never told you—and what they never wanted you to know—was that the Quiet Revolution was a period of intense cultural upheaval in Quebec that started soon after the elections of 1960. It had its origins in the decades-long indifference being paid by English Canada to the needs and expectations of ordinary Quebecers. Having a Catholic Church riddled with sex offenders only made matters worse. Merely seeking basic inclusiveness within the broader Canadian family, Quebecers felt like they didn't matter, that they didn't belong—and that they weren't truly appreciated for who they really were as a proud nation. The Canadian deck was stacked against them. Confederation was failing. This soon spurned civil unrest, overt acts of hatred toward English Canada, passionate calls for Quebec separation, and eventually, domestic terrorism through the violent actions of the FLQ. You wouldn't know anything about the FLQ because its existence as a terror cell within Canada has also been expunged from the history books by the Rideau Club culture. Had you paid close attention to the film *Die Hard* with Bruce Willis, you would have recalled that vault-robber Hans Gruber demanded the release of three FLQ terrorists from a Canadian jail as a way of stalling off the FBI. But you wouldn't of course ever recall that as a direct fallout of the Quiet Revolution, the FLQ had actually set off more bombs from 1960 to 1970 than Bin Laden ever did across the entire Western World. Their crimes are what caused Pierre Elliot Trudeau to call out the army and invoke the *War Measures Act*. It prompted his famous "just watch me" speech on the front steps of Parliament in 1970.

Soon tanks and rifled soldiers would be everywhere on the streets of Canada. But in the year 2020 we blind-eye boomers would exclaim, "I don't remember seeing that, Russ. Are you sure?" You see, it's an absolute medical imperative for us to bury our dark past. How else are we going to get away with passing a dying planet and a vagillion-dollar debt onto our grandkids? Besides, "Costco has a sale on T-bones and flats of carrot cake. Gotta get going, Rusty. Peace out, man."

So this was the cultural upheaval context within which my mother took her deviance to the next level. Not that Drummondville wasn't also an idyllic setting. It truly was. Blissful and heavenly too. It was the place where we lived in yet another pristine bungalow in yet another quaint middle-class neighbourhood. Our address was 121 Boulevard Gall, very close to a treed park and a sweeping-vista golf course on the west bank of the majestic Rivière Saint-François. There were no future premiers or Hollywood actors living nearby, but there was a whole mess of decent folks who were understandably angry at anglophones. From time to time, we referred to them as frogs, but they constantly called us *les maudits têtes carrées*—which was impolite Quebec slang for those God damn square heads. The first year we lived there things were quite tense, but as long as we all kept our heads down and acted polite we seemed to get through the day just fine. But by the second year—by the winter of 1963 to be exact—things got real ugly. In the middle of the night we would often wake to the sound of rocks and bottles being thrown through our front living room window. My father received constant death threats at work. I was held back from attending kindergarten—with the rationale that it was simply not safe for me to go anywhere without my mom. For years a Grabb family yarn circulated that there had been a cat who'd been gutted and hung by a rusty wire from the tree in our front yard. For my mother, all this was a Godsent. It provided exceptional cover for her to descend back into her established Etobicoke-strong pathology of oscillating between extended periods of endearing love and tender affection, and scalding hot anger. She would go months, often a full year being the perfect loving parent. Then suddenly she would fly off into this outrageous fit of demonic fury—but not before making sure all my siblings were off doing something else. Almost always it was triggered by people paying closer attention to me than her. Use of the phrase "Gorgeous George" was her absolute trigger word. Slowly over time—when I would have otherwise been in kindergarten class—she would call me into her bedroom and demand that I help her put on her underwear. All those days of touching all those disgusting panties, girdles, garter belts and brassieres traumatized me for decades. The sight of a Victoria's Secret catalogue still—to this very day—evokes a stark gag reflex the likes of which the Poison Control Centre would be very envious. With everybody paying such close attention to the war going on outside, nobody ever noticed that when she and I were home alone she eventually got around to demanding that I help her remove her underwear and pleasure her orally. I was 5. She insisted it take place in front of a mirror so she could verbalize aloud just how beautiful she was. If I didn't bring her to orgasm, she beat me senseless right on the spot. I soon learned that being really good at cunniligus made me a good boy. It would be a sadistic and repugnant imprint on my brain that would subconsciously drive so much of what I would do decades later as a tormented adult. I had no idea at the time that it—along with my future addiction to alcohol—would be the very thing that would trigger my catastrophic stroke at age 59 in downtown Victoria. When that speeding BMW came barreling down toward my face I prayed it would strike me dead—right on the spot. I was nowhere near that Dundas subway station back in Toronto, but I sure enough wanted to die. To the outside world I appeared to be that debonaire business consultant with a friendly demeanor and a long client list—forever busting out the corny dad jokes. To the voice of conscience sitting on my left shoulder I was that despondent child who derived his sense of meaning and purpose from inhaling merlot and 'pleasuring' that long list of feral cat women who'd been lining up to get some ever since Marianne and I went our separate ways in 2000. It would be another 10 months before I would work up the courage to ask Marianne to give me another shot. It would be another 18 months before I was back in her loving arms for good. I was 61. Sitting here now at 62—telling Reilly all about my life of enslavement—became the very moment when I started to feel like I might finally run full speed from that master bedroom in that pristine bungalow in that fucking majestic town of Drummondville, Quebec. Like I said, rabid-animal ugly. Scalding hot angry. And this is only the beginning. It actually gets far worse.

**CHAPTER 11:** Laughter and Soft Lies

ON MY NEXT VISIT to Reilly I told her that in the summer of 1963 my father had finally had enough of all the walking on eggshells. Concerned about the safety of his family, he up and quit his fat-salary job in Drummondville and moved us all out to Chaplin, Saskatchewan. It was a village with a population of 263 people on the Trans-Canada Highway halfway between Moose Jaw and Swift Current. There, he got a modest-paying job as a technical manager at the local Saskatchewan Minerals salt flats. Breathing a sense of relief, we all huddled together as a loving family in a tiny house located at 504 5th Street. In addition to my mom and dad, there was me and my two older sisters and my two younger brothers. For me, it was a true Godsent. With me going into Grade 1 at the tiny elementary school just down the street— and with our house being too small for my mother to scurry away potential sibling witnesses—it meant there was zero opportunity for her to manifest her established pathology. She left me alone for the full year we lived there. The irony was that when my dad learned that the local barber had tried to lure me into the back of his nearby house—in order to put his penis in my bum—my mother was the first to slap on her parka and threaten to go over there "right this very second" and kill the fucking prick. How dare he? How could he do such a thing, was how it all went, I think.

All and all that one year that we spent in Chaplin as a family was an undeniably pleasant experience. More than anything else, it introduced me to the notion of fight or flight through compartmentalization. While we hung out in our tiny hovel, catching tiny lizards in the yard, cooking special meals, and getting tucked in at night with funny Charlie the Horse stories, the outside world was absolutely on fire. Over in Vietnam a big war was raging, and lots of young American boys were being killed for no good reason. Over on the east coast of the United States the Boston Strangler was still on the loose and scaring the ever-living shit out of the entire city. Down in Harlem, black people—what

Grandpa Fred called darkies—were rioting and burning the place to the ground. We were told that some group of longhairs from Liverpool were taking the world by storm, but we really didn't know what everybody meant by The Beatles. We had lizards captured in glass jars, so we really didn't care. I was at home sick with the chicken pox the day President Kennedy got shot in the head. I called out, "Mom, come quick, that Jackie lady has ketchup on her dress, and some Walter Cronkite man keeps interrupting my cartoon shows on the TV." It was an American tragedy of epic proportion, so of course it became the sole obsession of Canadian kitchen table conversation from coast to coast for years to come. Canadian poet Leonard Cohen tried to draw some attention away that month by releasing a novel called *The Favourite Game*. It delivered a veiled autobiography of his lifelong quest to find inner peace and celestial meaning. It was trashed as being too detailed, too focused on his troubled youth, and too fixated on the role that a cavalcade of sex with feral cat women played in corrupting his destiny. Mr. Cohen would soon quip, "In Canada, people can't accept the fact that anything good comes out of their neighbour's house, this is a particular Canadian failing."

What nobody ever understood about our time in Chaplin was why I, at age 6, absolutely refused to participate in the skating pageant that my two sisters were helping to choreograph over at the local curling rink. Everybody thought it would be so cute to see me portrayed as one of three baby squirrels who would skate behind a mother squirrel played by an adult—all to the tune of *Then He Kissed Me* by The Crystals. All the parents present were very close to calling the Mounties when I ran away and hid under the bleachers for five hours. Everybody thought I might have been kidnapped. They had no bloody idea where I'd gone until I finally revealed myself. Nobody ever clued into the fact that the monstruous sight of a woman's nylon stocking being stretched over a carefully contorted wire coat hanger—in order to fashion a baby squirrel tail for my costume—caused me to shudder with the greatest level of primordial fear any youngster could possibly ever endure. To this day, nobody ever understands my vomitous aversion to ladies underwear. In fairness, how could anybody possibly know? This is Canada. Nobody ever really asks anybody anything unless it involves something irresistibly American.

As I progressed along with Reilly through several more therapy sessions, she eventually worked up the courage to ask me if I was still comfortable working with her on this journey of self-healing. She advised that she had a colleague who had a practice over in the Dundarave area of West Vancouver who might be better equipped to help me. I got the distinct impression she was starting to think that the magnitude of my childhood trauma had been so intense that perhaps I should work with someone far more experienced than her. I told her that I was happy to stay with her, and that she was giving me exactly what someone in my shoes only ever wants: for someone with a kind heart to actually listen! I said that it was like all those survivors of residential schools. They go their entire life being dismissed as liars who're seeking unworthy financial renumeration, or the return of some forested track of Crown land, when all they ever really want is for their fellow Canadians to stop and hear them out. I went on to say that I had recently come up with the acronym LAC to explain what I mean. I relayed that all we survivors ever want is for people to listen, to ask questions, and to converse with us about what we went through. Listen, ask, converse. You'd think it'd be a small gesture, but all I ever got from my friends were blank stares and the occasional lecture on how to turn poetic truth into Marvel comic-con tripe. All Indigenous peoples ever get are angry stares and never-ending lectures on how they should just shut up and conform. If Canadians could only give us just a few moments of their time—and a small measure of compassion—we'd all go away quietly and stop writing vitriol-laced memoirs and calling for commissions of inquiry. We'd have what we need to take it from here. I heard somewhere this was a particular Canadian failing. I could be wrong.

Before guiding me through the disclosure of what happened when my family moved to Bramalea from Chaplin in the summer of 1964, Reilly asked me to describe the socio-cultural context that existed back then. She said she was starting to see another pattern; namely that so much of what I had to say about my mother might be just as explainable and understandable through a socio-anthropologic lens as it would be through the psychopathy lens that she'd been trained to apply. She said she was intrigued by my assertion that the greatest motivator and vulnerability of the human race is actually our quest for relevance and belonging. She said it was not unlike the so-called 'attachment theory' of established psychology. Never one to pass up a chance to launch into one of my trademark soliloquies about the meaning of the universe and impending doom—of the kind that would prompt Alena Grabb to say "what ev's Dad" back in those delirious Coal Harbour days—I of course wasted no time sharing my thoughts. It was almost as if I was born to share this kind of unusual socio-anthropologic insight. It was almost as if this was shaping up to arguably be my true destiny. We would soon see.

It was billed as *the* most innovative urban design experiment in all of North America. Occupying almost 100 square miles of appropriated farmland just off the northwest corner of Metropolitan Toronto, Bramalea in the early 1960s was said to be the very first satellite city in the world. Located within the historically rural jurisdiction of Chinguacousy Township, before it was subsumed decades later by the nearby City of Brampton, its purpose was to provide the idyllic place for weary Canadians in the post-World-War-II era to peacefully raise a family and prosper in the unequalled economic boom that was then sweeping across the country. Built in phases with street names based on letters in the alphabet, it was to have the very best libraries, schools, parks, recreation, and retail and grocery shopping. The so-called indoor mall had yet to be conceived, so shopping complexes were merely called plazas. The first phase of affordable middle-class homes had street names that all started with the letter A. They were based in the A-section, with Avondale Boulevard being the epicenter of the initial design experiment. Soon came the B-section with names like Birch Road and Belmont Drive. A swanky Chatelaine home eventually got built up in the tony H-section. It was even featured in several glossy magazines. When you first drove into town—especially in the B-section—the first thing you would smell was the pleasant scent of French onion soup and cinnamon buns. It was simply divine. It was because just south of there, near the old Frasers Corners railyards, were the brandnew factories for Lipton Soups and Sara Lee Cakes. And just like the tried-and-true predatory model of the centuries-old Catholic Church, the whole urban design experiment was the ideal catch basin for vile sex offenders to prey at will on vulnerable children, under circumstances where middle-class, law-abiding, church-going and taxpaying eyewitnesses would have no choice but to look the other way—and engage in the favourite Canadian pastime known as willful blindness. You didn't need to be a socio-anthropologist to notice that not one single house in Bramalea had a double car garage. What sane person in the 1960s would ever think that a pie-baking housewife sporting an apron—who handwashed dishes and needed her spouse to co-sign cheques—could ever safely get behind the wheel of a car. Only men who had jobs and brought home the bacon could ever be expected to do such a crazy thing. A two car family? Like that'd ever happen.

Upon our arrival in Bramalea in the summer of 1964, my parents bought a four bedroom home in the B-section for $13,000. Stunned by sticker shock, they were sure they were never going to be able to pay it off. Our address was 30 Brentwood Drive. It was directly across the street from the new home of that renowned race car driver, Dennis Coad. He used to tell us all about that glorious time when he allegedly mopped the floor with Niki Lauda over in Europe. Up the street—about eight houses away—lived Andy Bathgate, the all-star right winger for the Stanley Cup winning Toronto Maple Leafs. A few years later, Mr. Bathgate would rent out his house to Orland Kurtenbach, who would later go on to become the very first Captain of the Vancouver Canucks. We actually moved there so that my dad could rejoin the car battery firm he left in haste one year earlier. They gave him another fat-salary job at their Toronto factory and promised him he would never again have to work in Quebec. Within a few short years he'd invented the iconic Sears Die Hard battery and was totally on fire across the corporate world. His boss's son—R. Dean Taylor—had a hit record down in the States called *Indiana Wants Me*, so of course there was lots of "America's the best" talk every night at the kitchen table.

So let's just be very clear. My parents and my parents' generation had just survived the Wall Street Crash of 1929, the Great Depression and the dustbowl famine of the 1930s, World War II, the Korean War, and now, with the advent of affordable automobiles, giant freeways, accessible commercial air travel, and something brandnew called colour television, they were all very anxious to get out there and wallow in *the* greatest economic boom that planet earth had ever witnessed in its long 4.5 billion year history. In the case of my own family, I had: an uncle who was seriously wounded while flying in a Lancaster bomber in World War II; a long dead grandfather on my dad's side who'd escaped the deadly purges of the Bolsheviks; and a father named after

Czar Nicholas who barely beat tuberculous as a child. Grandpa Fred and Grandma Margorie lived close by in London, while my Russian grandmother who was born in 1899—with the name Mary Kotovich—lived down in Windsor. For the longest time a Grabb-family yarn circulated that Grandma Mary put cardboard in her otherwise empty cabbage rolls during the Great Depression so my dad and Uncle Boris and Uncle Eugene could go to bed with full stomachs. We were all hiding behind the anglicized surname 'Grabb' to avoid it being revealed that my paternal Grandpa was a Russian immigrant with the ancestral name 'Grabov'. It was the perfect storm for everybody to take their eye off the ball. So anxious to put the past behind them and revel in all the splendor of Canada in the 1960s, nobody ever noticed that my mother was once again back to her old self. And she had plenty of cultural renewal cover within which to work. Nobody would be the wiser, and I would soon be a target of all her loathing and self-loathing. It all started right after Mrs. Coad said, "Oh my, your young fella there, Russell, he's so handsome." It descended into rank lunacy when all the girls in Grade 2 wanted to "go around" with me— and hang out at our house on Brentwood Drive after school. "Mrs. Grabb, can Russell come out to play?" became the new trigger phrase. Had they all been boy callers, things would have worked out much differently for me as a child, and frankly, later as an adult. As Jim Morrison of The Doors would have lyricized in 1967, this was "the end of laughter and soft lies" for me. The presence of pretty girls in pigtails and Buster Brown shoes circling like sharks with skipping ropes, radio flyer wagons, and chewing gum at the base of our driveway was what ultimately sent me tumbling down a path of irreversible damnation.

And speaking of eyes off the ball, this period in our splendid history was also the perfect time for the Canadian federal government to quietly ramp up its extermination of the savages. It was the perfect time to quietly load Indigenous children onto trains and buses and take them away to places that by any definition published by the United Nations down in New York would have been called concentration camps. Using the globally venerated Royal Canadian Mounted Police to do the dirty deed would make it even harder for other countries to catch on to all our cultural genocide. The sooner we 'boomers' could beat the Indian out of the child, the sooner we could all become more like our American idols down south. We couldn't have no God damn chugs and redskins walking around ruining everything. Racist to the very last coil of DNA, we sanctimonious Canadians just couldn't allow it. Catapulted to this glorious place in history by riding on the coattails of the now atrophied colonial British Empire, hitching our wagon to the American dream would be our last chance to secure our rightful place in the promised land of contrived economic privilege and felonious meritocracy. Those fucking Indians just had to go. Our Canadian addiction to willful blindness would be crucial. Anyone who ever dared question the propriety of a venerated mother out in Pleasantville would have to be eviscerated right on the spot. I believe in the modern age it's called being cancelled. I don't know for sure. I've been in leukemia cancer recovery mode so long I'm only now just catching up on the news.

So just as Brad Pitt spent those seven years in Tibet, I spent seven years in Bramalea. It was from 1964 to 1971 to be exact. It was a period that saw me go from Grade 2 to Grade 8. It was a time when once again my mother would descend back into her established pathology of oscillating between extended periods of endearing love and tender affection, and scalding hot anger. Once again, she would go months—often more than a full year—being the perfect loving parent. Then suddenly she would fly off into this outrageous fit of demonic fury—once again making sure my siblings were first off doing something else. Almost always her outbursts were triggered by other people paying closer attention to me than to her. Any reference to me being handsome or smart simply sent her over the edge. Any attempt by another female to get close to me was cause for war. Although she would sometimes get very cranky with my siblings, she strangely never had any trigger phrases or triggering events for them. Most of the time she was just a really good mom—and because I was so very little, and in need of so much nurturing warmth, I couldn't help but love her with all my heart. As I say, after a while I just couldn't tell the difference between appalling madness and a mother's tender affection. I just wanted to be a good boy. I just wanted to grow up and make her very proud of me. I did everything I could to please and win her ever-lasting admiration. Her ebb-and-flow affection was my lifeblood.

Now I'd be lying if I didn't admit that—for the most part—I experienced what most kids would say was a perfectly normal childhood. There were games, puzzles and toys. Hot Wheels and GI Joes were big favourites. There were hobbies and sports. There were swimming lessons. There were trips to the beach and really fun picnics. There were dixie cups and string to stay in touch— and tell your brothers the secret code. Heck, there was even full access to television shows and the odd special movie night out. At Christmas and on my birthday I was showered with an endless stream of special gifts and really nifty clothes. I could always go off to school dressed just like Bobbie Sherman, Davy Jones or Fabian. There was always tons of food on the table, lots of special meal nights, and loads of salty snacks with soda from the Pop Shoppe. I was living the Canadian kid dream. Early on I was enrolled in a pee-wee hockey league, and I soon played for a team sponsored by the Bramalea Fruit Market. I played goalie and even got my name in the *Bramalea Guardian* for logging two shutouts in a row. It's how I first acquired that CCM hockey bag that would soon play a rather scary role in my near fatal demise. I would be remiss if I didn't also mention all those times when my dad would use his company hockey tickets to take me to Maple Leaf Gardens to watch the Maple Leafs play the Canadians and the Black Hawks. Having a *Toronto Star* paper route also gave me direct access to Andy Bathgate's front door, under circumstances where I even once got to meet Dave Keon and Eddie Shack.

As a news junkie, I would read almost every single article in the *Star* before I delivered it door-to-door six days a week. This was indeed a historic seven-year period to be alive. It was a period that was peppered with no end of stunning current events and global tragedies. While we quietly lived our lives up here in Bramalea, the rest of the world was on fire. The Vietnam War just got bigger and bigger, and every night on the television news there were just so many clips of young boys being carried away in body bags and Viet Cong prisoners being shot in the head by some South Vietnamese General. Watching Bobby Kennedy and Martin Luther King get assassinated was nothing short of heartbreaking. Watching half the major cities in America being burnt to the ground by rioters was scary. My dad was trapped in Detroit on business the day it burnt to the ground and the Ambassador Bridge was closed off. Hearing that Air Canada DC-8 crash just a few miles away on that Sunday morning in 1970 was a sound no child should ever have to hear. We later learned that 109 passengers and crew had died. We all lost so much sleep when we heard that some guy named Richard Speck had murdered eight student nurses in a single night after herding them into a single bedroom over in Chicago. On the other hand, it was just so cool watching Ford roll out its new Mustang car. Watching all those hippies on the TV dancing like monkeys at Woodstock was such a gas. But the absolute highlight of those seven years was getting permission from my dad to shimmy up our television antenna and sit on the roof of our house the very day that Apollo 11 landed on the moon. I still get shivers down my back when I think about that sweltering hot evening in July of 1969 when we all gazed up at the stars. The FLQ were still bombing the fuck out of Canada, and closing down banks and Eaton's stores and such, but this wasn't America so nobody really paid much attention to it. Things were pretty quiet when our family visited Expo 67 in Montreal to eat buttery lobster at the Cuban Pavilion. It was even more cool being able to do so on a family trip to PEI. So much fun. So much tender innocence. So many truly happy memories to think about for many years to come. I really do miss playing on the monkey bars in the backyard with my brothers. Truth be told, they weren't stupid. They were my best friends. I loved them so very much.

And just as the glorious economic boom of the 1960s was peppered with stunning current events and global tragedies, my blissful childhood in Bramalea was similarly peppered with no end of criminal violence, sexual defilement, gaslighting, and a whole mess of demented lunacy. I know there was that cruel attempt to murder me in that shallow sink of water in 1965 because I had gone off to flirt with that pretty girl, Colleen, at the local Becker's convenience store. To this day, I still tear up every time I think of red licorice. Of course there was that time when I was hung by my ankles over that high balcony at the Holiday Inn on Riverside Drive West in Windsor during a family trip to go see Grandma Mary and Uncle Boris. To this day, I still can't go anywhere near fast flowing water. On a recent business trip to Whitehorse, I almost had to be taken to the hospital because my panic attack at seeing the Yukon River in full fury near my hotel was akin to what Tony Soprano experienced whenever he was confronted with the ghastly sight of bloody meat. There were of course all those unprovoked beatings—and times when my mother would sneak into my bedroom at night and force me to pleasure her. To this day, I still wake up in a gripping sweat at 3:10 a.m., ready to do whatever I must to fight back. To this day, I still keep my eyebrows bushy so nobody can see that jagged scar above my right eye. For years I was forced to say it was all my fault for tripping at the local IGA. I mean who the hell was ever going to believe that an apron wearing mother in a candy coloured house in utopian Bramalea in the '60s would ever order a young child to sit very still at the base of a staircase so she could repeatedly pummel him in the face. These of course were the things that would erupt with soul-crushing fury back on November 6, 2009, when Alena was on her deathbed. These were the things that made it seem like I too was in the process of dying at St. Paul's Hospital. No child should ever have to experience what it feels like to have their hair pulled back tight, and drowned face down in a sink of soapy water at the hands of their very own mother—while an empty unzipped hockey bag sits nearby calling out their name. I believe that if she hadn't slammed me onto the floor like a sack of potatoes, after being startled by the sound of my older sister briskly walking past on her way downstairs, I probably would have never jettisoned that tap water and regained consciousness. I would have been a dead corpse at age 8. I would have never had my chance to play more ice hockey, or go see a picture show with my friends. There would have been no retired RCMP superintendent publishing a jaw-dropping memoir about growing up in sunny ways Canada in the '60s to share with a bewildered world gone absolutely mad—just as he was turning the ripe-old age of 65.

I should add that the one beating that would later prompt this same superintendent to see his early-life trauma not as a sad tale of woes about his own plight—but rather as an abiding platform to convey awkward and ugly truth about the 'venerated collective' known as Canadian society—relates to that occasion in 1966 when he underwent conscious sedation surgery at the Brampton Civic Hospital to remove a 2" melanoma lesion on his lower back. Lying naked and face down on an operating table, he would yell out to the stone age team of surgeons and nurses that he could feel the scalpel cutting into his skin. Rather than injecting more local anesthetic, they would scold him for having the temerity to manifest excited delirium, instead of taking it like a man. They would rat him out to his mother waiting in post-op. She would promptly undo his hospital gown in front of all the nurses, toss him across her knee, and whip his ass with a leather belt ripped from his 9-year-old-boy corduroys—lying nearby on the blood-soaked floor. He would catch another beating from his dad for all the projectile vomit he would spew inside that luxury 1964 Buick Wildcat on the cozy ride home from the hospital. For decades nosy kids at the beach would ask him how he got that axe-wound scar that's still very much present on his lower back to this very day. When told the full story, they would all reply, "Cool." Clinicians conducting annual physical examinations would often ask, "Who's the ham-fisted butcher who put in those bad-boy sutures? Were you squirming like a dog at the vet when they went in?"

So ya, these are the kind of childhood memories that make even the most heartless prick squeal with revulsion. But honestly the very first thing that comes to mind for me when I think of Bramalea was that time when I'd come home from playing hockey—feeling nauseated and woozy because I had just been hit in the forehead with a puck. I was sporting a purple goose egg the size of a golf ball. In any other decade since it would have been classified as a Grade 3 concussion requiring hospitalization. But instead of running to my aid, my mother barked at me for being such a crybaby. She demanded that I help her put away the groceries. She handed me the peanut butter, saying, "There you go, honey. Put that away in the cupboard, will you?" After complying with her request, I got to work helping put the milk away in the fridge. Within two minutes she said, "Honey? Come here a sec. You know how I asked you to put the peanut butter over there on the counter, right?" I stood silent not wanting to offend. She continued, "Now do me a big favour and get it out of the God damn cupboard and put it over on the counter like I asked." Not wanting to end up with another fat lip, I once again immediately compiled. Two minutes later, she was back screaming, "Russell, God damn it. Are you stupid? This is the third time I've asked you to put the peanut butter away in the cupboard. Why is it over there on the counter? What is wrong with you? Honestly, I sign you up for ice hockey and buy you fancy corduroys so you can show off to all those stupid girls at school, and this is how you repay me?" In any other decade since it would have been classified as gaslighting in the first degree. It went on for another 20 minutes. It ended with me being punched squarely in the face and sent to my room with a bloody nose that I then had to crunch back into place myself using my own two shaky hands. I repeatedly threw up in my waste basket all day long.

The next thing that comes to mind for me about Bramalea back then was all the nudity. Featured front and center on our living room wall was an artist's rendition of a woman in what appeared to be romantic Scarlett O'Hara attire, with half her blouse pulled down so one of her shapely breasts could be displayed for the entire world to admire. That sultry dark woman in the painting was a dead ringer for my mother. It prompted kids in the neighbourhood to ask, "Why does your mom have a naked picture of herself on the wall?" At some point in time the painting was paired with a classy framed closeup photograph of a woman's eye staring at the blended reflection of a woman's naked ass. Every once in a while a Playboy centerfold would be scotch-taped to the door of the fridge—allegedly to give my perfectly proportioned mother motivation to lose weight. On those many occasions when my mother would lock herself in the master bedroom and cry non-stop for hours on a Saturday afternoon, she would often step out to check on me in my room, completely naked from the waist down. At one point I overheard her conniving with a neighbour to take turns posing nude for a local amateur photographer. The neighbour was that sexy Dutch woman who told my mother they could each make a lot of money sleeping with Bay Street millionaires who 'martini lunch' at the brand new Sutton Place Hotel near Queen's Park. When the family next door jokingly tossed me into their swimming pool with all my clothes on, my mother reacted by stripping naked in our kitchen, screaming, "How dare they treat my son like that? I'll show them." It took every ounce of strength for my dad to restrain her from leaving the house. It was a full on, hand-to-hand combat struggle. You needed an iron stomach to watch. It was a matter of existential survival for her to get out there and show her vagina to the world. And just like Rose Ann McKay, it was almost as if some mysterious childhood trauma was driving her to get even with whoever it was who hurt her so badly, back when she was young. I always suspected crazy Grandma Margorie. Maybe it was Grandpa Fred? Whoever it was sure as hell stirred up some rather sick monster psychopathy.

So by now you're probably wondering where was the father in all this. Father? Are you fucking kidding me? This was Canada in the sentimental 1960s. Fathers don't play a direct role in parenting; they go to work and drink highballs with their secretaries. Mothers stay at home and rule the roost with their manifest Olivia Soprano pathology. In 1971, when she softly sang, "My father sits at night with no lights on …. his cigarette glows in the dark," Carly Simon absolutely nailed the grim description of what it was actually like to live inside that Bramalea house. What about siblings? Ah ya, that. Well, they were off doing something else in the home, or over at a friend's place. This was Canada in the resplendent age of baby boomism. Nothing to see here. All good. Move along. Just a minor misunderstanding that's all. Bad things only happen over in Africa where all those darkies still live in huts in the jungle, you know. Have you tried the apple cobbler, Russ? It's truly to die for. You watching that new show, *Laugh-In*? So hilarious, right? It went on and on—and fucking on. Nobody paid any attention. Nobody gave a shit.

So if not a father, what about some sort of government child welfare service? Wouldn't they intervene? Again this was the Province of Ontario in the ever-resplendent 1960s. Elected officials didn't mandate that highly trained social workers steward over the welfare of precious children. They contracted that out to privately run groups of drunks and child molesters called "children's aid societies." Operated by Methodist churches and such, they were staffed by non-government laypersons who could be just about anybody off the street posing as a do-gooding intervenor. And when I say contract out I actually mean sluff off to some group of dirtbags who were always a full arm's length away from any sort of core government accountability. In 1960s Canada you could swing a dead cat and not ever hit anybody who actually cared about children. Everybody was just too busy spending money, getting laid, sporting miniskirts and bellbottom flares, driving muscle cars, and thanking God World War II was finally in the rearview mirror. The collective quest to be American, to emulate Peter Fonda and Mary Quant, and escape into a delicious new reality free of rationed shoes and butter, meant compassion for the vulnerable and the afflicted would clearly have to wait for another day. It was to be expected, right?

What my loving siblings never knew—and what they couldn't possibly ever understand because their snake of a mother had been so clever—was that every time we moved to a new home in a new town I was the only child to be given his very own bedroom. Everyone else had to share with a sibling. And just as the story that I had been denied entry into kindergarten in Drummondville for my personal safety was total bullshit, so was the assertion that Russell just has to have his own bedroom because he incessantly wets the bed at night. While it was indeed true that I wet the bed until I was 9 years old, the real reason I was given my own bedroom was so a sexual predator could have unfettered access to prey upon me. The real reason I was never sent off to kindergarten was so the same predator didn't have to go very far to hunt. It was the classic Catholic priest slash altar boy scenario. It's what prompted me to sleep in my pajamas while wearing my running shoes, naively believing I could actually run away if I had to. What my siblings also never knew is that the real reason their mother went out and bought an electric hair clipper wasn't so she could save money taking me to the barber all the time. It was because she and I stayed up late one night to watch a documentary on World War II, within which it was said that the reason all those Nazi collaborators had their heads shaved, after France was freed from the Germans, was to accelerate the degree to which all those traitors needed to be shamed for all their Vichy atrocities. Four days later my mother shaved my head bald and sent me off to school observing, "Let's just see what all those stupid girls think of you now, mister perfect hair." I was bullied for months by all the boys in the older grades for being that bald dork in floods. If you don't believe me, have a look at my Grade 5 class picture. I'm the broken soul with no hair—and pants sporting leg hems resting halfway up his scrawny little shins.

And speaking of Grade 5, that was the year when Mr. McConnell contacted my parents to inform them that provincial tests had confirmed their son Russ was somewhat gifted. I was to be kept in class during the day, but exposed after school to curated readings and expanded learning. I was soon handed books written by creepy looking guys in white sheets with names like Plato, Aristotle and Socrates. This was followed by assigned readings in Grade 11 math and Grade 12 physics. Field trips with Mr. McConnell and two other gifted students from Balmoral Public School included trips to Massey Hall to take in the symphony, and structured walking tours of Chinatown in downtown Toronto to understand how other cultures view the universe quite differently than us. It all went well until my mother realized that the other two kids were pretty girls. She pulled me out of the program, took away my books, and handed me the Bible. I read the bloody thing over a single weekend, but it didn't seem to make any logical sense. I thought the *Allegory of the Cave* by Plato did a better job explaining endemic human stupidity; something that would come in handy 50 years later when I was forced to work with assistant deputy ministers on contract at the B.C. Government. Despite my removal from the program, my mother grew increasingly more agitated with all the attention I continued to attract. The frequency of all her criminal violence, sexual defilement and abject lunacy reached an all new high. It prompted me to pack a pillowcase full of canned goods, slide out my bedroom window, shimmy down the television antenna, and make a run for the local railway tracks at 2:00 a.m. My plan was to walk all the way from Bramalea to Grandpa Fred's house in London following the CN rail line that goes there. He always told me my mom would one day come to kill me, so I better have an escape plan. As 10-year-old-boy luck would have it, I only got as far as Frasers Corners when I got hungry and realized I had forgotten to pack a can opener. I walked home in total shame, and was quickly subjected to no end of intensified beatings. To this day, Alena still ribs me for my habit of writing down all my daily chores on a post-it note the night before. To this day, Megan still mocks me for never leaving the house without two pens in my pocket. What they don't know is that my failure to bring a can opener that night imprinted upon my tiny brain this searing fear that if I ever again forget something important, I might actually get murdered. Like picking up lint and checking to see if books are stacked in alphabetical order, it's a habit I simply cannot break. My obsessive compulsive personality disorder, or OCD, will stick with me until my dying day. It's a matter of absolute existential personal survival for me. If I don't control the external universe, it quickly controls me. I soon experience unfathomable pain. To me, every failure in life is a forgotten can opener and another horribly broken nose.

A couple days after my failed runaway attempt, my dad told me he had arranged a tour for me of the local Chinguacousy

Township police station. I thought that would be so very cool. Like all 10-year-olds, I just loved firetrucks and policemen. I couldn't wait to go. When we got there I was immediately introduced to Constable 'Pete' who scared the ever-living shit out of me with his big black holster and his shiny black leather cross strap. Like that prison guard in the film *Midnight Express*, he was waiting with steamy bated breath. Bald, grossly overweight and sweating like a pig, he told my father to wait outside while he dragged me by the arm into a back room in what looked more like a B-section house than a modern police station. He told me that my dad had told him all about my failed escape and how it would be his job now to tell me what happens to delinquents who don't do as their fucking told, who question the sanity and propriety of their very own mothers. He made me aware that fathers who bring home the bacon needed to be shielded from intolerable shame. He showed me grotesque black and white photographs of adult men inserting their penis into the rectums of little boys no older than 6. He said the next time he saw me he would be taking me away to a reform school in Guelph so older men like him could royally fuck me in the ass until I turned 18. He asked me if I had any questions. When I said, "Where's Guelph?" he slapped me across the face and said, "Don't be a smart ass, you're no E.P. Taylor." In the coming days I told absolutely everybody who'd listen what happened, and what my mother had being doing for years. I told teachers, Grandpa Fred, neighbours—even my school principal and the burly Brampton cop who lived next door. All I got were blank stares and the occasional lecture on how Canadian kids need to just shut up and be thankful they're not over in Japan where children were starving. In 2019, when I was reading in the *Toronto Star* about the heartbreaking child sex abuse case of Kevin Dickman, I finally understood why any kid asking any Brampton cop for help in the 1960s was no different than a baby lamb asking a blood-soaked lion for a decent best place to sleep tonight.

So ya, when all you pious Canadians ask, "Why didn't you say anything at the time? Why didn't you fight back, Russ? Why didn't you run away?" I'm here to tell you it's not like all those tone-deaf Netflix movies. In the real world it's an actual form of institutionalized enslavement. All your neanderthal Canadian ancestors in the 1960s simply stepped right over my culturally accepted desecration. They of course did this on their way down to that fancy new indoor mall called Yorkdale to buy pricy bellbottoms and outlaw sunglasses. It was a classic Canadian trait they would pass on to you so you could simply step right over the Downtown Eastside on your way to downtown Vancouver to buy pricy jeans and gangster hoodies from some clothing store over on Robson. Wanna know why it took me over 60 years to say something? I've got just one word for you:

Guelph.

Fucking Guelph.

Just having to type the word in this moment brings tears to my eyes. How could these heartless people do such things to such a good little boy? I just wanted to grow up and make my mom and dad proud. I just wanted to be an architect and have a nice family. I just wanted to be a good husband, a good dad. I never wanted Rose Ann McKay to stab me to death. I never wanted to watch Alena die. I never wanted to make it to a place where there would finally be a chance at attaining inner peace and celestial meaning only to learn I had incurable leukemia.

---

So before we continue on with my disclosures to Reilly about what I endured as a child, how about we just stop and consider the optics here for one second?

The broken child who you pious Canadians threw to the wolves in the 1960s turned out to be the very person who David Milgaard would call in 1997 to ask who he and his mom Joyce should call in order to demand a public inquiry into his wrongful conviction for murder—now that DNA evidence had exonerated him. It's true that the Tragically Hip had written a Top 40 song about his plight called *Wheat Kings*, but it would be a Sergeant Russ Grabb who he would call because he had seen me on the television news talking about the Air India bombing and the Clifford Olson faint-hope hearing out in Surrey. He thought I seemed like a really nice guy. I listened. I asked questions. I conversed with him. I gave him the names of some high-profile lawyers who'd previously done good work dealing with these types of things.

On June 23, 1985, when 268 Canadians—including 83 vibrant children—were savagely killed in what still remains the largest mass murder in Canadian history, it would be a Sergeant Peter Montague who would be asked to be the lead media spokesperson in order to explain to the world how such a horrific crime could possibly happen within Canadian jurisdiction. And long before the very talented Corporal Catherine Galliford would become the indelible media relations face of the Air India bombing investigation, Sergeant Montague would pass the public communications torch onto the very person who you self-righteous Canadians threatened with sodomy and pedophilic imprisonment if he ever again dared to question the blessedness of the pristine Canadian delusion. Coincidentally, when Sergeant Russ Grabb was in a green room in Vancouver at 4:00 a.m. in November of 1998—waiting for a 7:30 a.m. EST appearance on CBC Newsworld to discuss Air India—sitting right beside him was none other than former NHL star, Sheldon Kennedy. Sheldon was there with his spouse to discuss his recent cross-country roller blade trek to raise awareness for the true extent of pedophilic predation across Canada.

In April of 2020, when a psychopath masquerading as an RCMP officer gunned down 22 civilians in Nova Scotia, it would be that same terrified child Russ Grabb who would quietly contact several top news anchors across Canada to remind them that it was actually Air India, not Portapique, that was the scene of the largest mass murder in Canadian history. Desperately ill with leukemia, the little scamp still had the strength to politely point out this gross error in basic journalism. He knew it wasn't because of journalistic incompetence. He recognized it was because of the Canadian tendency to always forget about repugnant crimes committed against non-whites and non-Christians right under our very noses. You see, in Canada every barbarity almost immediately becomes a Macarena dance. Rehearsed outrage fills the first block of every television news broadcast for days on end—and pots and pans bang on balconies for weeks—then suddenly it all dies off as if it never even happened. Just ask that Islamic faith family down in London how quickly their family massacre story disappeared from the minds of mainstream Canadians, right after all our virtue signaling ran out of steam. Just ask the Coquitlam aunt of little Alan Kurdi; that 3-year-old hopeful Canadian refugee who was found lying face down and heartbreakingly dead on a lonely beach in 2015. Within hours of Russ Grabb's gentle nudge to top news anchors covering the Portapique story, newsrooms everywhere were quietly tweaking their breaking-news copy.

Are we thinking about the optics here?

In 1998, when Ross Rebagliati won that controversial gold medal at the Winter Olympics over in Japan, who do you think was asked to go up to Whistler on short notice and explain to Canadians what the official Canadian government and RCMP position was on cannabis? Little monkey-bar climbing Sergeant Russ Grabb would get summarily hammered on email the very next morning by all his RCMP colleagues across Canada for daring to suggest on television that it was perhaps time to assess sensible options for decriminalization, if not outright legalization.

When the leaders of 21 nations, including China, Indonesia, and the United States, came to Vancouver in 1997 to attend the global APEC summit—and when the whole deal turned into a giant dumpster fire of civil unrest, police overreach and charges that a sitting Canadian prime minister had ordered a crackdown on lawful dissent—it wasn't that same prime minister, or even his most senior spokesperson, who went on television night after night for two years to clean up the bloody mess. The person on *Canada AM* live with Dan Matheson, explaining the inexplicable, wasn't Commissioner Murray or Minister Anne McLellan. It was of course some hapless schmuck called Sergeant Russ Grabb who once delivered the *Toronto Star* newspaper on his banana seat bicycle way back in 1966, only months after being drowned by his mother.

When DND needed an experienced investigator to travel over to the Canadian Embassy in Kyiv in 2001 in order to look into the expense irregularities of the naval attaché posted over there, they sure as hell didn't dispatch the likes of Constable 'Pete'. When the Secretary General of Interpol that same year scoured the planet looking for a skilled detective to sort out what the hell was really going on with an FBI agent, *The London Times,* and suspected nuclear arms smuggler Grigori Loutchansky, he sure as hell didn't yell, "Get me that Brampton cop turned Baptist minister who repeatedly raped Kevin Dickman in the '60s just a few blocks from where Russ Grabb grew up in Bramalea." When the Canadian Armed Forces Provost Marshall needed somebody to visit the Supreme Headquarters of Allied Powers in Europe at NATO in Belgium in 2000—in order to serve formal papers on a warrant officer charged with the sexual assault of a female subordinate— she definitely didn't ask for some homicide investigator hanging out with strippers at the Marble Arch back in Vancouver. In all instances there was no room for all that "laughter and soft lies" that kept the pristine Canadian delusion going in the 1960s. This was serious business. There was no room to phone it in either—as would have been the case with that Bramalea land developer who went bankrupt not long after its faux Camelot project cleared escrow and all the original investors were off living pampered lives in giant castles on Georgian Bay. In all instances, they absolutely insisted upon the proven expertise of Inspector Russ Grabb; that same beaten down, emotionally eviscerated and wretchedly tormented rascal who once only made it as far as the Frasers Corners railyards in the middle of the night.

You getting the picture?

You left him to suffer.

Immeasurably so.

Then you sent him off into the world asking that he grow up to become the only human being on planet earth to ever put in jail one of the rapist psychiatrists from the Allan Memorial Institute at McGill who helped develop the brutal tactics that were used by the CIA in the 1950s to torture the Unabomber when he was then just a plucky 16-year-old worrywart child studying mathematics at Harvard University.

You broke him.

Ya, you.

Nobody else.

You.

You and your continuing addiction to willful blindness and your pathetic open worship of all things shallow and flawed. It's the very reason you're clinging to your fucking smartphone right this very second. It's why you just can't wait to check your social media feeds before spin class this afternoon, isn't it? It's most certainly why you and 40 million other Canadians openly idolize that jackass from Stratford who once defaced Anne Frank's diary and callously bragged about it on Facebook.

You broke him.

You broke him, but he never stopped fighting.

He never stopped trying to prove that he too mattered, that he too belonged, that he too could be loved for who he really was as a person.

Paul Bernardo ended up a serial killer, and Kevin Dickman ended up taking his own life in the frigid waters of the Don River, but somehow that scrawny kid from 30 Brentwood found a way to crawl forward.

With more chemo sessions waiting for him just over the horizon, I suppose it's just how it was always meant to be.

# CHAPTER 12: 32 Wind Sprints

AS I STARTED to wind down my time with Reilly, she eventually came around to say, "Okay, Russ. I've connected the dots as to why you mailed that ill-fated letter to your mother in 1977, when you were still studying at Ryerson. Those of us who study the childhood trauma spectrum understand that blaming oneself and idolizing the abuser is quite common. It's to be expected. It's nature's way of allowing the survivor to sidestep shame and despair. All that you've disclosed here so far has allowed you to mostly come to terms with everything. We're moving in the right direction. You're on a path of sustainable healing now. It's really heartening to watch. But to put a wrap on our work I'd like to explore a bit more of what happened with you in high school, after your family moved on from Bramalea. I already know how and why you ended up with the French Foreign Legion RCMP in May of 1977, so this should be the last piece of the puzzle at which we should probably have a closer look. Are you good with that?"

So yes it's true that my whole family moved to Guildwood Village in Scarborough in the late summer of 1971. It was so my father could be closer to his new workplace up near the 401 at Markham Road. Our new address was 154 Catalina Drive. Once again it was a four-bedroom house with a quintessential middle-class Canadian appeal. Once again I was assigned my very own bedroom, while all my siblings were required to double up based on gender. Three houses away—just over that old backyard fence— lived preteen and future serial killer, Paul Bernardo. During the ensuing five years that we lived there—ranging from 1971 to 1976—I first attended the much acclaimed Sir Wilfred Laurier Collegiate Institute high school. For Grade 13 I moved over to West Hill Collegiate Institute. Being a tried-and-true Scarbeerian, I of course embraced the local '70s lexicon later shared with the world by fellow Scarbeerian, Mike Meyers; a lexicon composed of locally evolved phrases like party on, no way, hurl, and are you fucking mental? Three decades later some youngster named Abel

Makkonen Tesfaye would also attend West Hill Collegiate and swap out our lame overwrought lingo for something a little more current, a little more fire, a little more slay. He would of course do so after changing his name to The Weeknd. It would be a moment in our history when aging boomers would exclaim on all their Facebook pages just how resplendent life was growing up in utopian Guildwood Village in the '70s. It would be crammed so full of grand pristine delusion, you'd soon be hearing *Sugar, Sugar* by the Archies wafting off all those screenshots. They would of course redact any reference to Paul Bernardo on Sir Raymond Drive, to the child molester living in those creepy apartments on Livingston Road, to that 3" layer of green scum and dead fish floating down the street on Lake Ontario, or to the French teacher who ran off with that smoldering hot teenage girl in his home room class.

So asking me what the hell happened during this period is kinda like asking whatever happened to John Travolta between *Welcome Back Kotter* and *Pulp Fiction*. Much of what had been going on in Bramalea continued to play on, but the intensity and tempo of all the madness fell way back. My mother carried on with her demented gaslighting and tortuous mind games, but after we moved there she never again touched me sexually or attempted to beat me in any way, shape or form. It was still living hell being trapped in that house—and certainly thoughts of suicide grew ever more intense—but it was refreshingly different. Years later I would chalk up her shift in behaviour to the arrival in 1971 of our adopted baby brother, Lloyd. He was the cutest little guy. Smart as a whip too. His presence in the home changed everything. It gave my mom a project into which she could pour all her energies and exclaim even louder, "How could you say such a thing? I'm your mother. I give my life to you kids on a silver platter, and this is how you repay me?" It was almost verbatim what viewers would hear coming out of the mouth of Olivia Soprano in Season 2 of *The*

*Sopranos*. To this day, I'm still convinced she was wearing a wire for David Chase. I also believe the huge fall off of criminal violence and sexual defilement had a lot to do with the fact that I bought a set of dumbbells from Simpsons-Sears in Grade 9, and built myself up to look much like a young Jan-Michael Vincent. When I heard Pierre Elliot Trudeau say "just watch me" I knew just what to do. Neither she, nor any older bully kid down at the park—or over at school—were ever going to fuck with me again. In fact, in Grades 9 and 10 I took great pleasure pounding the ever-living shit out of any punk—no matter how big or mean—who even looked at me sideways. At four-foot six inches and 120 lbs., I was the most feared scrapper in school. With the earned nickname Grabber, it wasn't long before I was also a force to be reckoned with out on the football field. Fourteen years of simmering anger were channeled directly into the chops of every motherfucking prick who ever got in my way.

Looking back now I would have to say there were probably six factors that kept me from going insane in high school. Firstly, I poured myself into academics. I studied hard and did my best to get good grades. I wasn't always very successful because my emotional mood continued to wax and wane. Next I poured myself into athletics. I wasn't very big, but I excelled at tackle football, wrestling, track and field, and competitive gymnastics. Getting an after school job at McDonald's was also significant. Even as a teenager I was being groomed for bigger and better things, and I even once got to meet the founder Ray Kroc who came to my Eglinton store in a Bentley driven by Canadian CEO, George Cohen. It was so cool witnessing Mr. Kroc say to me, "Where you from soldier?" Immersing myself in the 1970s McDonald's corporate culture gave me access to friends and warm comradery far removed from school and my own family. It was so much fun hanging out with fellow teens after work—often until five in the morning at the local Fuller's restaurant near the iconic Knob Hill

Tavern. Little did I know that Mr. Fuller and his sons would one day launch numerous successful restaurant chains with catchy names like Earl's, Joey, and Cactus Club Cafe. Little did I know that one day I would proudly father a gal who'd end up being groomed for executive leadership prominence within the Cactus Club Cafe chain. Of course there were the lyrics of all those Top 40 songs like *Someone Saved My Life Tonight* by Elton John and *Paint It Black* by The Stones into which I would escape. But most of all, the big thing that kept me sane—and allowed me to beat back all those terrible suicidal ideations—was being able to hang out in high school with that older kid, Terry Mercury. Terry was my true hero. He was a star athlete and a lettered student who just had this extraordinary knack of treating everybody with such great kindness and authenticity. In the locker room at the gym, or out on the football pitch, he always had words of wisdom about life and living that rivaled anything any decent father could ever hope to muster up. He was the man. At the end of every grueling football practice Coach Baker would make us all do 20 wind sprints. It meant after we had just completed an exhausting full-contact practice session we would then have to do 20 back-to-back sprints across the width of the football field before hitting the showers. Terry would keep on going and do an additional 12 for a total of 32 wind sprints. I would stay with him and do exactly the same thing. It was Terry's way of teaching me to never give up and to always go the extra mile. If I'm not mistaken, I believe he's now some sportscaster dude over at SiriusXM. His biggest advice to me was, "Grabber. You know. I gotta say. If you haven't gotta whole mess of blood, grass, and mud stains on your jersey at quitting time, then you weren't really in the game." At the time I took this as a tip about playing football. I now know he was busting out one of the most prophetic metaphors anyone could have ever shared with me. With me now grappling with my mortality, it's certainly good to know that no matter how hard the socio-anthropologic forces of a willfully blind and tone-deaf Canada tried to smother, if not outright kill me, I just never quit. Although admittedly misguided by my own calamitous sense of obligation to the celestial universe, I had always been in the game. I believe the indelible spirit of Terry Mercury had been there with me the whole time. Without that rather rare, un-Canadian gesture of compassion I'm not sure I would have made it to my 16th birthday, nor gone on 50 years later to write *the* seminal Didionesque essay on *the* most gigantic class-action delusion ever perpetrated by a single nation in the post-industrial era of human evolution. I'm talking about a provocative truthteller called *Traces of a Boy*. If you don't believe me, just ask the hundreds of Indigenous people still staggering about the forlorn streets of the Downtown Eastside, still looking for their parents—still using every grain of fentanyl they can get their hands on to suppress the unbearable pain memory of criminal violence, unlawful confinement, sexual violation, institutionalized malnutrition, third world healthcare, cultural and language eradication, and even medical experimentation and murder committed against small children all across Canada in the sentimental 1960s. It's something to think about when you're surfing in Tofino on our very first National Day of Truth and Reconciliation. It's especially true if your father was actually the Minister of Justice and the Attorney General, and later Prime Minister, at the very height of the '60s Scoop. It's even more true if—despite all the fawning over at the CBC—you weren't actually the prick who coined the phrase "sunny ways" and you pinched it from Sir Wilfred Laurier without ever truly understanding its sexualized double meaning.

# PART III:

When one man comes to his
final moment of clarity ...

# CHAPTER 13: Snakes and Ladders

LIKE ALMOST EVERYTHING in my life, I remember it like it happened just yesterday. It was an episode that typified a reality that still haunts me to this very day; namely that serving as a senior executive in the RCMP—at any level—is always such a soul-eviscerating experience. Commissioner Giuliano Zaccardelli was coming over to use the auditorium over at the Canadian Police College where I was then posted as the superintendent in charge of the police sciences school. It was the spring of 2003, and I was in deep discussions with the Canadian Association of Chiefs of Police as well as the Canadian Police Association which represented police unions from all across the country. Together, we were collectively looking into the best way to revamp and modernize our major crime investigation and major case management training programs. With there being so many police services struggling with rampant organized crime, cybercrime and homicide-investigation challenges, it was vital that we got this right. It was a true pleasure working with so many chiefs of police and union reps on this file. I felt like I was making a real difference to public safety on a national scale. The last thing I needed was this pompous jackass Zaccardelli—or Zac as he liked to be called by his sycophants—coming out here and throwing me off my game. It reminded me of that time in 1984 when I played the conscientious objector card up at Whistler Detachment and boldly stated my refusal to travel to Vancouver to join the throngs of RCMP sheep who would be throwing in on the close quarter protection of Pope John Paul II. As you may recall, he was in town visiting for who knows what fucking purpose. After what I endured as a child, the very last thing I was going to do was join in on the class-action worship of the world's most insidious gang of criminal pedophiles. My supervising sergeant in Whistler said, "Okay, Grabb. Not sure what this is about, but I'll approve it. You stay back and mind the fort while the five of us head down to the city. We'll be back in two days, so no funny business. If you need backup just give a holler to the boys up in Pemberton."

So ya, Zac in 2003. He had just spent the last two years euthanizing the much popular and most effective community policing policy of the RCMP, replacing it with some convoluted tripe he called intelligence-led policing. It was his way of insisting that reaching out to citizens in order to build good will, earn trust, and jointly solve public safety problems in unison, was a sign of hairy ass Mountie weakness. It was his way of ensuring that federal enforcement nobs from Ontario and Quebec could finally be treated with just as much respect as real RCMP cops working out in all the other 8 provinces and 3 territories. Any member of the senior executive who disagreed with his mantra and his iron-fist control of the Force was summarily banished or forced into retirement. It kinda reminded me of my rookie years in City South in 1977 when we were all told that anyone who disagreed with the imposed narrative of the brass was to be drawn, quartered, and arrested under the "stunned cunts act." He was coming over here today to give yet another one of his look-at-me speeches to an indentured audience of commissioned officers assembled from all across the Ottawa region. My bet on the office pool among we few contrarian types was "six and Denise." By this I meant Zac would say, "I am the Commissioner" exactly six times in his short speech—and Denise from Corporate Services Directorate would most likely be the person in the audience to whom he would direct all his overwrought oration and brutally awful jokes. I know it sounded like such a silly thing for such high-ranking people to do, but could you really blame us? Now I can't say he ever engaged in anything that rose to the level of open or unwanted flirtation, but everywhere Zac went he would incessantly remind his audience that he, and he alone, was the Commissioner. It often seemed like he was looking directly at just one person in the room. With a mug that looked like Barney Rubble, and a frame that resembled Fred Flintstone's, it was just his way of working the crowd. He didn't throw red ball caps into the audience, but he sure as hell reminded me of somebody. I can't quite put my finger on it, but I'm sure it'll come back to me in time.

I wasn't in any position to play the conscientious objector card this time, so I just called in sick and worked from home. Turns out I lost the office pool to some Inspector who correctly guessed "eight and what's-her-name from Finance." No biggie. At least I got out of having to listen to the little tyrant describe how he would soon be taking the Force down a path to where the Brown Commission would have no choice in 2007 but to call Canada's much storied Royal Canadian Mounted Police a despotic organization with a horribly broken staff culture. Efforts to make the RCMP '1950s again' would soon backfire. No biggie. My heart really wasn't in this easy-touch Ottawa job any way. Where I came from, we homicide investigation types operated on the 72-72 principle. It was the notion that if you can't button down in 72 hours exactly what the murder victim had been doing in the 72 hours leading up to their death, the chances of ever solving the bloody thing were next to none. It meant going 72 hours without sleep: kinda like a surgeon or an intern at a modern hospital. It was just something you did no questions asked for the greater good of Canadians. It was how Daniel Craig solved the disappearance of Harriot in *The Girl with the Dragon Tattoo*: he found photographs of the girl at a parade in the 72 hours leading up to her big vanishing act showing her react with stark fear to something quite innocuous in the crowd. He worked non-stop for another 72 hours until he and Lisbeth put a wrap on the case by killing the villain and reuniting Harriot with her uncle. Sitting here now, being forced to work such lame 8-hour shifts, five days a week, with weekends off, was a real step backwards for me. I felt bad for all those general duty constables working the graveyard out in Red Deer. I was worried about my homicide investigation buddies still working the salt mine out in B.C. They were all still having to do real policework out in the real world while the rest of us management types just complained the photocopier was out of long paper and Taco Tuesday was no longer on the menu down at the cafeteria. The only thing that kept me going through all this bureaucratic tedium was being asked to create and chair the National Council of Investigative Excellence that was comprised of a blue-ribbon panel of criminal investigators, investigative journalists, social-justice academics and lawyers from all across Canada, one of whom was the Assistant Deputy Attorney General who struck that unfortunate deal with Karla Homolka before those bloodcurdling video tapes finally revealed that she was fully complicit with Paul Bernardo in the unspeakable torture, rape and murder of those three teenage girls.

While it was true that I was a high-paid superintendent living the high life in bullet-safe Ottawa—and while it was true that I'd just come back from France where I'd given a talk on major crime investigation training to a delegation of French-speaking African countries—I was done. I was a fish out of water, and it was time for a change. I was done being the white sheep of the RCMP. I had arrived at the Canadian Police College the very day that Al-Qaeda struck the World Trade Center—after I had just spent two grueling years down at the Department of National Defence rooting out criminality at the highest levels, and being placed directly in the crosshairs of all those pious Ottawa types who 'martini lunch' down at the Rideau Club over on Bank Street. I guess it was to be expected. After all, the Rideau Club had been founded by the architect of Canada's residential school system: the ever-revered Sir John A. MacDonald. I guess it was expected that I would be next up to be smeared and teared. After all, in two short years down at National Defence I had overseen the global investigation of 330 criminal cases and the commensurate laying of 120 statutory charges. So there I was again. Just like Bramalea in the 1960s: daring once again to challenge the sacredness of the pristine Canadian delusion. They came at me hard with commissions of inquiry, ombudsman investigations, professional standard reviews, and even urgent calls to the Deputy Attorney General of Ontario to question the integrity of my investigations. It was like being an FBI agent loaned to the Teamsters Union in the 1970s to clean up corruption. Once you start doing a good job, guess what happens next? As I travelled daily across Canada it wasn't uncommon to be greeted by news crews upon my arrival who knew my exact flight itinerary, who arrived preloaded with got-ya questions fueled by leaked false information fed to them by shattered-ego senior commanders over at DND HQ. For Heaven's sake, they even tried to indict me under the *Officials Secrets Act* for using the wrong fax machine to copy my boss on an approved press release already released to the public. If I hadn't shared my affidavit on the Matt Stopford mutiny case with Peter Worthington—the ever-revered Editor Emeritus of the *Sun* newspaper chain—I would have been a goner. In my very own Pentagon Papers moment, I was able to reshape the narrative and beat back all the coordinated smears. I ended up being branded as a competent criminal investigator and a man who was not afraid to stand accountable for his very own actions. Although initially his sworn enemy, Worthington would eventually write of me in two successive full-page editorials that, "Military justice is to 'justice' as bagpipes are to music, yet before Grabb's fine leadership our military police seemed hellbent on finding whatever results the higher command wanted. His meticulous and detailed affidavit seems a model for how an investigation should be carried out." I guess it also helped that I pulled a bit of a Tony Soprano stunt by conferring with one of the lawyers who would have otherwise been engaged by all my litigious detractors, thereby rendering him in conflict and unable to work on their behalf. The jaw-dropping Johnny Ola moment of all this Kafkaesque madness was that day when that lawyer said, "Man, am I ever glad you came to me first. I just can't stand these cocksuckers. Sure they pay well, but man, what a bunch of insufferable dickheads they are." He wasn't referring to Mr. Worthington, but he was very specific in his direct reference to that venerated cathedral down on Bank Street that they all love to call their special blueblood home. I once joked that if Hollywood were to script a movie about this phase of my life it was going to have to be called *The General's Fodder*. When two former CBC television reporters were hired by DND to question my handling of the media during this tricky national stage assignment, they made all the chain of command heads explode when they reported back that how I dealt with journalists, conversed with the public, and exercised sound crisis communication, was a textbook example for everyone else to follow.

When the military faction of the Rideau Club culture grew weary and ran out of options to nail me to the cross—simply for doing my job of sending entitled upper echelon shit heels to the brig for breaking the law all across the globe—they called in a bunch of favours down the road at 1200 Vanier Parkway. Some panting Deputy Commissioner asked Superintendent Jim Brezovski to comb through all the commission of inquiry findings and ombudsman reports to find any tidbit that might support *Code of Conduct* charges against then Inspector Russ Grabb. Being an incorruptible chap with a law degree, Jim reported back that I was the Wayne Gretzky of criminal investigation, and a man who should be touted as the very model of integrity for everyone else across the Force to emulate. Ironically, it had been then Constable Jim Brezovski who gave me a lift back to North Vancouver RCMP Detachment when my patrol car was fire bombed in City South in 1978, when I was just an upstart constable. On the drive back, I told Jim I'd pay him back by being the first to back up his girlfriend, Constable Adrienne Moncrief, whenever she had to go toe-toe with one of those entitled upper echelon shit heels from Argyle High who were known to take great pleasure breaking the law all across the North Shore after gym class—all while driving the trust-fund Chevelle they got just last Christmas from daddy.

In the spring of 1999 Solicitor General Lawrence MacAulay announced that the federal government would be spending $115 million to modernize the CPIC computer system used by law enforcement agencies all across the country to track criminals and investigate crime. Part of the announcement was an assertion made by RCMP Assistant Commissioner John L'abbe that $32 million would go toward the launch of a new national index system that would cross-reference arrests, prosecutions, sentencing and parole data so that never again would Canada witness the kind of fiasco that unfolded when child murderer and serial rapist Paul Bernardo was on the loose back in the late '80s, early '90s. A post mortem of the Bernardo case suggested that in part he was able to elude police forces in Ontario for so long because of the inability of those different forces to pool information and cooperate effectively. Assistant Commissioner L'abbe informed the CBC in 1999 that "the reason users wanted a national index is to prevent things like the Bernardos." In September of 2003 Superintendent Russ Grabb was summarily yanked from his cushy position over at the Canadian Police College in order to take over the then 4-year-old national index project and find out why the hell $22.4 million had been spent by contracted IT vendors on building nothing more than a simple one-to-one relational index that did absolutely nothing to advance the noble cause of public safety. It was a useless piece of software that could have been fashioned together by a 6-year-old over a single weekend at the cottage using Grandpa's IBM model 5150 personal computer and Aunt Mabel's grocery list file on her Blackberry. Treasury Board analysts were furious. They wanted answers yesterday. Needless to say, I was pissed right off about this assignment—and not just because there had been so much rancid incompetence. I was pissed because it would mean my desire to return to Vancouver as the superintendent in charge of a homicide investigation team that would one day become known as IHIT would be yet again delayed. If I didn't get back out west soon, I may never get the job. It would probably be given away to some rising star like Wayne Rideout.

For me, finding out what went wrong with that national criminal index investment was like that 6-year-old finding out there's no Santa, no Tooth Fairy and no Easter Bunny. I learned that despite what we non-tech mortals think, professionals working in digital-tech are actually dumber than day-old pigs. They bombard us with all their convoluted lingo and acronyms and dress sloppy not because it's their way of doing things, but because it allows them to throw us off the scent of their rank stupidity and their overpaid salaries. We think they're all geniuses. We revere them, if not fear them because we think we could never do what they do. It's their schtick, and the firms for whom they work all have what I call the 'tapeworm business model'. It's the notion that you get deep inside the host organization—either a government agency or a business like WestJet—leveraging an idolized brand. Once there you suck the host dry of all its financial and inspirational nutrients, never enough to kill it, but always enough to create a dependance on over-priced management consulting services and completely unnecessary IT. The way to spot an IT project that's doomed to fail—and they all almost always do—is to look for the phrase "cool and trendy." The reason I mention WestJet is because six years later, on November 6, 2009, when Alena was on her deathbed and Marianne was doing her level best to scramble out to Vancouver before it was too late, WestJet would deny her basic service not because they had done anything wrong, but because some IT vendor had hornswoggled them into buying a cool and trendy reservation system that would reportedly make WestJet the envy of the entire airline industry. On day one of its launch—on

November 6, 2009, to be exact—it crashed. On day two it crashed. Two weeks later it was still not working properly. Eventually it had to be scrapped, resulting in a $30 million write down and the departure of a CEO. Were it not for the charity of Air Canada who placed Marianne in seat 1A at no extra charge—so she could be first off the plane upon her arrival in Vancouver—we're not really sure if she would have ever survived that agonizing 5-hour flight. Poor Marianne cried non-stop the whole trip out. To this day, she still thinks about that wonderful flight crew who extended her so much kindness and moral support. To this day, I still think about how much I hate IT vendors and everyone who venerates them like they actually know what they're doing. After what they just went through with that "cool and trendy" Phoenix pay system, I'm pretty sure there's 302,000 federal government employees across Canada who would agree with me on this. The IT vendor in that instance was none other than the globally venerated, revered and idolized firm known as IBM. Back in my formative youthful days—back in 1971 to be exact—The Poppy Family sang that evil grows in cracks and holes, but it didn't take me very long as an adult to realize that it actually flourishes in the delusions of humanity. Our collective longing to sidestep immutable truth and worship liars has, and will always be, our calamitous downfall. Our desire to matter, to belong, and to be loved for who we really are makes us easy prey for the lying-in-wait forces of contrived corporate branding and scurrilous click-bait tech—and oh ya, sex offenders, serial killers and overrated piece-of-shit celebrities too.

When I met with the Treasury Board analysts I passed along my opinion that there had been three huge mistakes made with respect to this $32 million project. Firstly, the RCMP had been assigned to act as 'prime' when in fact this was a federal government venture. I reminded them that although year-after-year surveys show the RCMP with a 92% approval rating among Canadians, we Mounties in fact have the lowest Balanced Scorecard rating of any department or agency in government. I stressed that when it came to digital-tech, we were the very last agency who should ever oversee something of this nature. We're an organization who thinks Windows is something you stare out of, and JavaScript is an exotic recipe for coffee. Secondly, despite a clear delineation of what the actual problem was, the RCMP and all its tapeworm cronies treated this as an exercise to design a software program, as opposed to what it actually was: a real-world undertaking to design and stand-up a government program. In other words, this was supposed to be a $32 million investment in a modern business operation that would bring together all police, law enforcement, corrections and prosecutorial agencies in Canada under one brick and mortar roof, under circumstances where accountable governance and cost sharing could be collaboratively devoted toward shared public safety outcomes, as opposed to electricity flowing through some server down in the basement. Finally, I passed along my view that it was a huge mistake to contract this work out to any of the so-called "big five" consulting firms. I shocked the room when I informed them that I had discontinued our relationship with the lead IT vendor and had gone off and pushed through the procurement of a competent team of business architects from CGI. I ended the meeting by laying out my bold plan to meet face-to-face with public safety and justice officials from all across Canada, at all levels, in order to build consensus, earn trust, and agree upon shared interests and measurable outcomes. With everything I'd endured as a child, with all I'd seen out west as an actual homicide investigator, and with Paul Bernardo being my backyard neighbour as a teenager, I was in no mood to take any guff off any propeller-head policy analyst. Nobody said a word when I shred the fourteen PowerPoint presentations and scrapped the single-index programming language for which the taxpayers had just coughed up $22.4 million. In Ottawa if you forget a can opener—and screw up something really important— you get promoted to assistant deputy minister. In my world, you get beaten senseless and shipped off to Guelph for years of sexual defilement. In my world there's absolutely no room for the "clinician reconsideration" of serial rape. In my world, the immutable is never debatable. In my world, there's no room to say, "Look, Russ. We all come at these things with our own unique cultural perspective. There are no right answers here." In my world, you either achieve the correct outcome or innocent people die and entire Indigenous communities go without potable water and slowly decay into spiritual-hope oblivion. It's kinda why I'd never, ever, graduate from MBA school. I just seem to have this rather annoying fixation with essential outcomes, versus cool and trendy, yet almost-never-effective management practices. I'm the only one observing that universities everywhere have replaced the quest for consequential knowledge with fashionable drivel. Every subway station in the world is plastered with posters prompting our children to set aside Plato, Descartes and Einstein, and go get a useless MBA. It's places like Ivey, Royal Roads, and Rotman where emerging corporate world snakes and RCMP executives get indoctrinated into the notion that flawed processes and useless tools are their indelible tickets to ladder climbing.

So you may recall that I once said I finally rounded out my three decade career with the Mounted Madness by perfecting crime reduction models and disaster and pandemic response programs. This occurred between the spring of 2004 when I was gratefully transferred off that silly IT project and sent back to Vancouver, and June 12, 2006, when I commenced my RCMP retirement and my glorious entry into the private sector. You may recall I left the Force on a Friday and started work the very next week, on a Monday, as a fat-salary executive consultant with CGI. It was my oversight of the business architecture for that noble federal government venture that got CGI all fired up about headhunting me to come join their team. I never did get the job overseeing that high-profile homicide investigation crew, but I was pleased that in the two years before leaving the Force I did have the pleasure of working with then Assistant Commissioner Gary Bass and Professor Darryl Plecas from the University of the Fraser Valley on launch of an innovative approach to harm reduction and street policing that led to double-digit crime rate reductions at six pilot sites. Our collective effort led to the rollout of chronic offender intervention pilots all across B.C. It was when I'd been asked to serve as the *ex-officio* Chair of the Division Executive Committee, or DEC, that oversaw all RCMP operations across the region. My very last assignment before turning out the lights and heading out the door was to write the business case to fund a new modernized approach to emergency management and pandemic planning; something that better positioned the RCMP and the B.C. Government to respond to natural disasters of Katrina hurricane and Indonesian tsunami scale, and prepare everyone for any unforeseen catastrophe—including domestic and foreign terrorism—related to the 2010 Winter Olympics coming up in just four short years.

So ya, what a bloody career that was. I was 49 years old, and here I was heading off into the sunset as just another net present value millionaire. It remains the greatest secret ever kept by any group of practiced whiners anywhere in Canada. We Mounties always complain about being so overworked and underpaid, yet if we simply put in 24 years or more of service, like I did, we always collect a platinum-plated pension with benefits that are far more lucrative than any Member of Parliament ever gets. As my old homicide investigator buddy Doug Hartl used to say, "If members of the RCMP ever worked to rule they'd have to come to the office twice as much." All we ever have to do to collect our seven-figure annuity in retirement is live well into our sixties and beyond. We're the only group of lunch-pail workers I know of who can fly off into the blue with a winning Scratch & Win ticket in their back pocket after only 24 years. Don't ever let any retired RCMP officer tell you how hard done by they are. When it was my turn to move on I was offered the usual disingenuous retirement dinner, going away party, and gifts from the officer's mess. I turned them all down. I just wanted to step away and get on with my exciting new challenge out in the private sector. Fucking Zaccardelli was still the captain of our floundering Titanic ship, so it just seemed wise for me to quietly disembark at Iceland before our vessel of misogyny and ineptitude got any closer to the Newfoundland coast. I had made the list for promotion to chief superintendent, but I just didn't want to be part of the impending implosion of the Force. Yes, that Old English font parchment bestowed by Her Majesty in 1999 allowed me to use the title "Sir" whenever I was in my commissioned officer uniform. Sure, if I'd only been able to hang in there for seven more years I probably would have been promoted to Assistant Commissioner. But it really stung knowing that the Director of the FBI stateside had issued me a commendation in 1998 for exemplary efforts, yet my very own Commissioner up here absolutely despised me. The landscape was becoming ever more gloomy. Exceptional detectives like Bob Paulson and Gary Bass, and forward-thinking leaders like Bev Busson and Janice Armstrong, were all a dying breed. Almost every underperforming dolt across the Force was being invested as a Member of the Order of Merit. It really was time for me to go.

What heartened me most as I stumbled out the door—without ever having received any medal for my work overseas in places like Lyon, Kyiv, Manila, and Brussels, or even for my bravery going hand to hand with a knife-wielding Rose Ann McKay back in 1979—were all the expressions of affection I received from all the down-to-earth people with whom I had been working. Lloyd Plante—himself an astute major crime investigator—said, "I'm really sad you're leaving, Russ. You're just not like the rest of us." Gerry Peters of the Native Indian Residential School Criminal Investigation Task Force said, "If God forbid anything bad should ever happen to any one of my kids, you'd be the only guy I'd ever want working on the case." Detective Brian Honeyburn from VPD, who had been working with the RCMP on the Unsolved Homicide Unit, said, "You can't leave, Russ. You're the only Mountie who knows what he's doing." Now that was a true compliment. Witnessing any veteran member of VPD ever say anything nice about *any* Mountie was like hearing Don Cherry ever say anything nice about a Finnish hockey player who wears a visor. It just never happens. And long before I approached my retirement years, I also once received an unsolicited email from the exceptionally talented media spokesperson, Corporal Catherine Galliford, stating that in her ongoing review of solved and unsolved murder cases—related to the Robert Picton serial killer investigation—she'd come to believe that I was, in her view, the one of the best investigators in the Province of B.C. As I made my exodus from the RCMP, I wasn't completely certain I'd achieved all of my French Foreign Legion objectives. But Lord knows, deep down, I was terribly dejected Marianne was still very much gone from my life. Sure, I had Megan and Alena living the gilded high life with me—way out here in Coal Harbour. Sure, I was swimming in no end of elevated wealth. Yes, I would soon have a polished Porsche permanently prepositioned at the Helijet base over in Victoria and a Buick Lucerne town car parked back over here on the mainland. No doubt, I would soon spend all my days off shopping at Leone and Restoration Hardware. But it really wasn't the same. Something was missing. Something big. Arguably now more traumatized by my time as a senior executive with the RCMP—than all the events of my entire childhood combined—I spent months self-medicating with buckets of medical merlot red wine trying my darndest to figure out what the fuck it was. Still that 8-year-old boy grappling with the unfathomable from back in the day, it turned out to be so much harder than I thought.

Then it hit me. I was sitting alone in a booth at an Earl's up on Broadway, bolting down yet another bottle of Rodney Strong. Seated directly across from me in another booth was Jann Arden—also alone, also fighting back tears. I knew she said she had a good mother, but I never really believed that could ever be possible. In that sad moment of reflection about my mom it hit me that whatever I was going to do next with my life would be calculated to find everlasting love again. Surely to God there was another Marianne out there somewhere. Surely to God, I wouldn't fuck it all up again. You can see where I'm going with this, can't you? I was an absolute genius when it came to solving complex cases and rescuing off-the-rail government programs, but when it came to matters of the heart, there was just something terribly wrong with me. It would take the writing of this memoir for me to finally figure out what it was. It would take the sudden jolt of imminent death from kidney failure, a full pancytopenia melt down of my entire immune system, and late-stage leukemia cancer during the first shocking wave of COVID-19 to finally fix it—but not of course before I lived and breathed the very darkest side of predatory females whose psychopathy and physical attributes felt eerily familiar. For some reason I just wanted to please them—and show them what a really good boy I was. It would take me into a downward spiral of catastrophic chaos and agony the likes of which even Alena's near death experience in 2009 couldn't compare. It would be a tale of extravagance, sexual debauchery, vomitous alcohol abuse, and inexcusable stupidity the likes of which even Mathew Perry could never surpass. You'll forgive me if, in sharing the details of this downward spiral, I once again resort to levels of vitriolic anger the likes of which no average Canadian—certainly not Jann Arden and the like—would ever normally tolerate. By now I'm certain you would agree it's any wonder I'm still alive to tell you about it, in any event.

**CHAPTER 14:** Keep on Lovin' Me Baby

IN NORTHERN IRELAND, during the period of savagery that took place between the IRA and the British Army from 1960 to 1998, it was called The Troubles. Between January of 2000, when Marianne and I sadly went our separate ways in Ottawa, and May of 2018, when we happily reunited for good in Victoria, that 18-year period of not dissimilar savagery could have only been described as The Disaster. Sure, it was true that initially I was that jet-setting RCMP Inspector, travelling the world investigating no end of criminal malfeasance within the Canadian Armed Forces. Yes it was true I travelled to Europe through Heathrow six different times in the month of August 2001 alone. Yes I did indeed get to stay in some five star hotel in London that one time when I had to swing by Brize Norton Air Force Base to seize contraband spirits being smuggled into England by Canadian peacekeepers posted over in Cyprus. Sitting beside software billionaire Michael Cowpland in business class on the way over was a real gas. Coming back with *Hello* magazines and Belgium chocolates for Megan and Alena from every trip was always loads of fun. Meeting and later becoming pen pals with that Versace salesclerk in Paris who'd—just three weeks earlier—personally sold Jennifer Lopez that plunging green dress with which she shocked the Grammys in 2000 is a tale that I'll one day have to tell my grandkids. I was wearing that black Versace cashmere coat she'd sold me when I had my near-death stroke in Victoria on January 5, 2017. And yes, later going on to become that unusually successful business consultant based in Coal Harbour was of course a huge milestone for me. But honestly, getting involved with all those women from one end of the country to the other became the biggest mistake of my entire life. That's right, in the 18 years that Marianne and I were apart, I managed to get myself senselessly mixed up with an array of romantic interests. And that doesn't even take into account all the others with whom I went out on one-night dates on a shamelessly casual basis. So whether it was that pharmaceutical rep from Toronto who I met at the baggage carousel at the Halifax airport—who had dinner with me later that night at the Four Points—or those two inseparable ladies way out west with whom I spent a weekend of fine dining at Whistler, these were all self-inflicted mistakes that would soon cost me dearly. It was all part of my perfectly understandable effort to recapture the sense of untroubled peace and gentle intimacy I once knew with Marianne. It proved to be the disastrous consequence of my quiet quest to win the approval of romantic interest women who subconsciously reminded me of my mother.

On my second-to-last mental health therapy session with Reilly in 2019, she asked me to get into a little more detail about what went on with me during this turbulent 18-year period. She said, "Russ, there's a sensitive subject you've been avoiding since we first started working on your healing journey. You know full well that your later-in-life interactions with women are key to understanding your childhood trauma, yet you always sidestep talking about them. I'm wondering if this is something we can get into here today? Looking through my notes I see that you once said something rather interesting about the acronym, LAC. I'm ready to listen, to ask, to converse, if you're good with that, Russ. Yes, that's right, LAC. You ready, my good friend?"

To this daring assertion I said, "Until I hear some living breathing human being actually utter the words 'Oh my God, Russ, you poor bastard, is there anything I can do?' I'm really not comfortable saying anything about all the women who came in and out of my life during this period." Reilly responded, "Why not?" I said, "Well, firstly all the keyboard warriors will swoop in and cancel me into oblivion. They won't take a single moment to understand that 'I too' am an actual survivor of actual childhood violence and sexual defilement by the opposite sex. They operate in a universe where men are born guilty, and women are born oppressed. They'll never stop to reflect on the fact that I devoted my entire adult life to hunting down rapists and men who murder women and small children. Next, I'll get hammered by the overwhelming majority of people out there who will say that I'm just some braggart misogynist who can't get beneath ego, who just wants to paint a picture that he's some sort of stud in bed. Then I'll get inundated by all the pig misogynists out there who won't connect the dots that my proclivity for a certain archetypal female is actually sound scientific indicia of an underlying predisposition to please and win the adulation of a long lost and always just out of reach parent. They'll treat my endless stories of wild incandescent sex and batshit crazy banter in blindfolds and leather as the 2019 version of the 1982 version of Penthouse Forum. I'll get hit with pig-male comments like, 'Did you cum in their face? Did she take it up the ass? When you had all those threesomes did they ever go down on each other?' They'll turn my quiet quest for thoughtful reflection and peaceful healing into a sexoteric playground of over-the-toilet masturbation. Finally, I'll get labeled by all those completely tone-deaf academics who will sanctimoniously opine that this is clearly a case of an Oedipus complex, wherein it appears 'patient Grabb' harbours a clinically deviant obsession to have sex with his mother. I'm not Jim Morrison from The Doors. I may one day write a song called *The End*, but rather than seeking to have sex with my fucking mother and kill my fucking father, my childhood proclivity has always been to run just as fucking fast as I could in the other fucking direction. If the fucking human race could just stop thinking they have all the fucking answers, and—without ever fucking listening, ever fucking asking, or ever fucking conversing—know without absolute definitive fucking certainty what's actually wrong with me, then maybe I'll have something meaningful to say about all this." Reilly replied with a smirk, "Russ, you poor bastard. Is there anything I can do?" Finally, a scientific breakthrough in my quest for safety and inner peace. After 62 years, a fellow Canadian was finally respecting immutable truth. As I peck away at the keyboard—crafting this very memoir—I'm wondering if her family ancestry may have had something to do with her unique insights into psychology. You know what Sigmund Freud allegedly said about the Irish, don't you? Either way, it's clear Reilly was impervious to the carcinogenic Canadian assault on all things awkward and true.

———————

So ya, back in 2006, after I finally escaped the Shawshank prison that was the globally revered RCMP, it didn't take me long to get underway full steam with my exciting new career at CGI. I was only there one year before starting my own company out in Vancouver, but I was able to sponge up everything there was to know about management consulting proficiency and digital-tech investment planning in government and out in the much rarefied corporate world. I even got to learn a little about software programming. To my great "Santa is dead" regret, I specifically learned that despite how all these propeller-head types market themselves, almost none of them actually know how to write software code. The big secret they never let on to us non-tech infidels is that all they ever do is sew together apps and patches of software already written years ago by actual coders; apps and patches that are free for the taking on almost all open source forums out there in this completely overrated and much full-of-shit IT universe. Had it not been for Leslie Lamport in the '70s, and his insistence on use of actual mathematics, the whole digital-tech world would come crashing down in one calamitous implosion of fakery. When I launched my own firm in 2007, I thought to myself this is going to be like taking candy from a baby. You had the entire human race believing that IT vendors and digital-tech gurus actually know what they're doing. You had assistant deputy ministers and C-suite executives out in the private sector absolutely clueless as to how to run an organization or lead people. As Albert Einstein once said, "Perfection of means and confusion of aims seems to define our age." By this he meant that anybody with an MBA from Rotman, Royal Roads or Queens thinks it's the tool, the technique, the methodology, the approach, and the cool and trendy framework that matters most, and that results, outcomes and acquired insight are just things for another day. All their collective effort meant that with the complicit help of the management consulting profession, everybody out there was just busy making all the wrong things go 'better, faster, cheaper'. Everybody was busy becoming highly proficient at doing all the wrong things sooner, with greater consistency, and at less cost. Folks were constantly counting how many times they brushed their teeth every day instead of measuring just how white they were becoming. It was all about celebrating targets with no outcomes. It reminded me of the Trudeau government in the 1970s: celebrating the on-time, on-budget and on-plan construction of the Mirabel airport. Billed as the biggest, most modern, and most opulent airport in the world, zero airplanes ever really landed there— statistically speaking. As I headed off to run my own firm I knew the secret to instant success would be to do the opposite of what all my peers in the industry would do. In fact, my elevator pitch was simply, "We're not Deloitte." From what I saw back in Ottawa with the RCMP, and from what I experienced firsthand at CGI, I knew that hiring anyone with an MBA to serve in any essential leadership role was the same as giving aspirin to an infant with Reye's Syndrome. At first glance it appears to be the ideal solution to the perplexing problem, but suddenly it causes instant death. All their 'people-fear-change' mantra was so far out of date you could actually hear the soundtrack from *Pretty in Pink* wafting off the slides of all their PowerPoint presentations. Anybody like me who had actual life experience, where it actually counted, who suggested that people actually fear being abandoned, ignored, and devalued, was simply dismissed as being a crazy heretic.

So after leaving CGI in 2007 I was definitely successful, but all of my engagements were being delivered through other consulting firms on a sub-contractor basis. I would land the sale, but they had the pre-established billing infrastructure and insurance coverage to make it all happen. But by early 2008, I was ready to bust out completely on my own. I had already made my first million—hence my purchase of that gold Rolex watch—but now was the time to wear the big boy pants, and go do it all on my own. With Megan still in Grade 12 at King George just down the street on Denman near Stanley Park—and with Alena not far behind in Grade 10—I was ready to work my magic. I came up with the idea to pitch my services to a wide range of federal and provincial government agencies, highlighting that through my unique expertise with conducting current-state assessments of floundering pre-existing government programs, they could save millions of taxpayer dollars by spotting and rectifying big problems before they unfolded with embarrassing calamity on the frontpage of all the national newspapers. Serious about actually winning a contract, I was careful to never mention my prior history as a senior executive with the RCMP. Despite their very own addiction to tapeworm assisted failure, my clients were all aware of the shameful Balanced Scorecard track record of my former employer. Letting it be known that you once served with the RCMP was like telling a group of hedge fund investors from Wall Street that you used to be the top guy at Nortel, Myspace, and Blockbuster.

After a couple of months of making the mother of all roll-the-dice cold calls, I finally got a hit. I finally got a call from a senior executive working at a high-profile federal government department. She had a swanky corner office just three blocks away on Burrard Street, just up from the Harbour Air floatplane station in Coal Harbour. She said she was most interested in what I had to offer and would be pleased if I could submit a proposal to conduct $25,000 worth of initial scoping on a current-state assessment for a large government operation in the Pacific Region. She scheduled multiple meetings to discuss her steep requirements and expectations. She initially had her full team present, but as time progressed the attendance just got smaller and smaller, and eventually, it was just she and I meeting privately. Being the doofus teenager from Scarborough that I was, it took me awhile to notice that as time moved along she began to wear less and less clothing. By the time we scheduled our final contract sign-off session she was wearing nothing more than a leather mini skirt, stiletto heels, and a tight-fitting and low-cut sweater that made her look like Anita Ekberg from the movies in the 1950s. Sure she was very attractive, but I was narrowly focused on winning the contract, and more importantly, on getting the job done correctly so taxpayers wouldn't have to fund yet another huge public sector disaster. I asked, "When shall we sign the contract and move forward with procurement?" She replied, "I was thinking we could discuss that tonight at my place over dinner. I have this cute little condo over in Lower Lonsdale overlooking the ocean, right next to the Seabus terminal. No need to bring any wine. A toothbrush is all you're going to need. You mentioned once your daughters are in high school, so no need to arrange a sitter, right? Do you mind if I put shallots in your scrambled eggs in the morning?" When I asked, "What about the contract?" she replied, "Oh Russ, you're so pretty. I thought you knew. There never was going to be any contract. Our department doesn't have those kind of discretionary funds. Are you kidding?" We were sitting side by side at a conference table, so it didn't take much effort for her to place her right hand on my inner thigh right up by my crotch, and say, "I thought you understood, Russ. This whole contract proposal was just something I cooked up so I could get you in the sack. You looked like one of those male Abercrombie & Finch models from the 1990s that day you swung by for your first cold call visit. Is 7:00 p.m. good with you? I'll put on *Bawitdaba* by Kid Rock, maybe some *Keep on Lovin' Me Baby* by Colin James. We can fuck like a couple of crazed teenagers."

Well so much for Lower Lonsdale girls in skirts and heels who listen to Air Supply—who pine for lasting love with a good man. This was some crazy fucked up shit. Think about it. Was there really any difference between asking, "What about the contract?" and "Where's Guelph?" Either way, it was a stinging slap across the face from a fucking pig sporting an I-have-all-the-power-now-bitch uniform. You see, whether it's a black leather cross strap worn by Constable 'Pete' in the 1960s, or just some tight-fitting sweater on a predatory female hunter in the modern age, it's all the same diff, isn't it?

⁓

When I pressed ahead with the final leg of my healing journey with Reilly she eventually got around to saying, "Okay, Russ. Enough with the ducking and weaving. Tell me specifically about these love interests who came in and out of your life in the 18 years that you were apart from Marianne. I know enough already to conclude that we are really talking about a proclivity affliction, versus a sex addiction condition. If this had anything to do with sex addiction there would have been 'round-the-clock masturbation, non-stop porn watching, escort services, and casual intercourse with complete strangers. You would have had frequent bouts of chlamydia and syphilis. There has been no evidence of any of these things. If anything, I see a patient who constantly ends up in the throes of unhealthy relationships because of an unconscious desire to please and win the admiration of an archetypal female who once made you feel safe, whose pathology feels warmly familiar, who once taught you there's no real difference between abuse and affection. Where I think you might be slightly off in your self-diagnosis is your belief that these females hunt *you*. The literature on these types of affliction suggests that it's not a matter that they seek you out for predation, but rather you offer yourself up to them of your own free will, most often without ever realizing the consequence of your very own actions. This isn't to say you're to blame. It's more that, by no fault of your own, you've been injured by your mother, and without intervening therapy and serious self-reflection, you'll continue to equate pain and degradation with affection and approval. You're very lucky to have Marianne back in your life. What do you call her again, my earth angel, or something? Without her, you'd have a hard time ever finding that safe place that you've been searching for all your life. But don't worry. You're almost there. You've come a long way. You should be proud. Tell me about these women, Russ. We both know who most of them really represent, don't we?"

I was ready. Finally ready. If the outrage cartel wanted to excoriate and cancel me now, after all that I've been through, after everything I've endured, then so be it. If my own siblings want to come on the attack in defence of their mother, then all the shame will be on them, not me. I was a good man who did his level best under difficult circumstances to live a good life, a peaceful life. It was my time. It was my turn. I replied to Reilly, "I guess I should first apologize for all the f-bombs, right? Not being believed, not being listened to, and always being labeled as something you're not is a gazillion times worse than being sexually violated in the first place. You can't image the anger that I feel right now." She nodded in the affirmative. She knew.

I carried on by saying, "If I may, I think it's important for me to share 62 years of context before getting into the cringeworthy detail that you seek. Let me start off by saying that in our culture, in our society, there's this notion that only men have hyper-erotic libidos. In our world we blindly accept the falsehood that only men watch porn, and only men talk dirty in bed. We all embrace the delusion that girl-on-girl sex, and threesomes with two women, is the exclusive fantasy domain of drunk and oversexed college boys. We assume only men grope the opposite sex in the workplace, and that only men use positions of power, or weaponized attraction, to groom the opposite sex as potential prey. Most notably, and I can say this with total personal experience clarity, we assume that only men cheat on their partners. Look, the only difference between men and women is that men are pigs. They brag incessantly to their homies the very moment they cheat, whereas women are discreet. They take everything to their grave. They say nothing to their best friend. Nothing to their mother. Nothing to their sister. Nothing to their co-workers. Absolutely nothing to anybody."

Reilly said, "I can see that. It comes up a lot in my discussions with my female patients."

I continued, "I know all this stuff not because I'm some sort of snooty armchair socio-anthropologist. I know this from personal experience. Sure, there were lots of Sadie Hawkins types in high school, always looking for every chance to take their clothes off. And of course there was that married English teacher who told me and that Italian immigrant boy Enzo that she wanted us both to "take her" together in the faculty lounge. But it mostly all started right after Rose Ann McKay tried to slit my throat in 1979. I foolishly ran off and got involved with a coke snorting nymphomaniac who spoke incessantly about girl-on-girl sex, who introduced me to every crazy erotic rabbit hole you could ever read about in Penthouse Forum. If I'm not mistaken, she's now a senior vice-president at one of the most high-profile corporations in Canada. They're in the news all the time. She once blindfolded me in bed, and without ever asking my permission, rubbed cocaine on my gums until I got super high. I often wonder if she stills sings 'no one knows what it's like to be the bad man' in the shower every morning. It was her absolute obsession anthem—and her get out of jail free card—back in 1979."

She gasped, "You did cocaine as an RCMP officer when you were 22?"

"Reilly, you have no idea what kind of shit I got into in my life. Have you ever seen that movie *Alfie* with Jude Law? Well, I'm ashamed to say, that was me. In my early twenties, right after that nympho dumped me for that girl in her ballet class—long before I met Marianne—I fell into this sad pattern where ninety percent of the women with whom I had playtime in the bedroom were married. They were unrelenting. They always made the first move. They almost always had the same opening line. They almost always started off with, 'I had a dream about you last night, Russ.' They always had the same lame rationalization at the ready. They would always say, 'I love my husband, but this is just something I need.' Over time they would always frame their infidelity as being no different than going to the spa. For them, it wasn't cheating. It was like getting their nails done. It was something they absolutely needed in order to stay sane in their highly stressed married lives. As I said, relentless. In North Vancouver in the early days they would say, 'Let's have sex in the office,' or 'Bill's suiting up for an ERT take down of five terrorists up on the Squamish Highway tonight. Apparently they bombed a cruise missile factory back east and two porn shops over town, so he won't be home for a while. Why not pop over for a pajama party?' Married women who I met while attending night school at SFU would say things like, 'Let's ditch these books and go somewhere really cool and fuck. Rick's away on business in Calgary so he'll never know.' Married women who reported house burglaries would often call me back to the scene of the crime on the pretext of having realized more jewelry was missing. Upon my return, they would often be wearing nothing more than a nightgown. Within a few minutes of small talk about the delinquents who would commit such crimes, they would quickly switch the conversation and make their move. One with whom I had dinner at the Keg 'n Cleaver in Lower

Lonsdale demanded that I take her on the hood of her husband's 1979 Corvette. When I asked, 'What about scratches to the paint,' she slapped me across the face and said, 'Shut up and just fuck me already.' Up in Whistler they would say, 'Let's head down to the city for a dirty weekend. I'll bring the MDMA and the Twister board so we can get totally fucked up.' Down in Richmond they would often break into my house half naked. There was even that time when I had to wake my roommate up in the middle of the night so he could help me eject that married next-door neighbour who'd climbed through my open bedroom window wearing nothing but a pajama top. Yes, naked from the waist down just like my fucking mother. Not much different really than that other neighbour who waltzed in my front door in her terrycloth robe, which she then quickly dropped to the floor revealing that she was completely naked underneath. She hit me with that ever lame icebreaker line, 'Does this shade of lipstick make my hips look fat?'"

"And all this crazy making stopped when you met Marianne?"

"Fucking right it did, but not before a close friend's wife made a huge play for me when I was over in England in 1985 for a friendly visit. Her ploy was to feign an ankle injury at the British Museum of Natural History, hoping I'd carry her back to her hotel room on Baker Street for a naughty sleepover. She soon labeled me a basket case when I summarily turned her down. It drove home the point for me that these weren't dysfunctional women, or women in lost and lonely relationships. These weren't highly promiscuous women, or women with clearly defined psychiatric issues. Nobody was ever drunk or stoned either. These were just women. You know, married women. Married women of all ages, all demographics, all religious persuasions. Over pillow talk they would all complain that they felt trapped in a universe where it was impossible to ever explore their natural erotic side without being labeled a whore. They thought it was so unfair that men and red carpet invite women got to have all the fun—while they're stuck having to quietly masturbate under the covers. They'd say I was their perfect pixie dust escape valve because I was bad boy enough to light their fire, but always too busy worrying about doing the right God damn thing back at the office to ever turn into one of those slimeballs they'd all read about in those Jackie Collins novels. Goldilocks wanted porridge at just the right temperature. These married women wanted sugar and spice, but almost always, nothing ever nice."

"Were you ever worried what some husband might do, if he ever found out?"

"No, but I bet you there's well over thirty women today who're praying to Christ I don't rat them out in some tell-all book. Their fear won't be that their affair with me was finally made public. Their fear will be that it will become known that they, in each and every case, made the first move, and had to employ some pretty clever tricks to wear down my initial resolve to say no— clever tricks they know historically are only ever attributed to misogynistic pig men."

Thank God I never told Reilly about that married woman in 1983 who was six months pregnant, who absolutely insisted that I "take her from behind" on the orange shag rug in the living room of that low-rent walk up in Marpole—that she was housesitting for a friend. Reilly surely would have canceled me as client for that one. Like I said, relentless. Bloody relentless.

So ya, now, with all this background about my demented life as a single man in the early '80s, I'm sure you'll understand why I had absolutely no hesitation saying no thanks to Anita Ekberg and her tight-fitting sweater. I mean the nerve of her. I put in 40 hours of non-billable time crafting what I thought was the most brilliant client proposal ever written in the history of management consulting. I even had Alena help me tweak and improve upon my PowerPoint presentation. I was so proud of what I'd come up with. I kinda felt like that child who comes home from school and his parents don't even look twice at his diorama project that just won first prize in some grade school contest. I was so disappointed with the failure to even consider all the effort I'd put in that it actually took me several weeks to realize, holy cow, I've just been played. Then it finally hit me. This senior executive from that federal government department was completely comfortable with using me in order to have sex. It's not a matter that she was merely looking for romance and saw me as a potential mate. She ended our conversation with, "Don't take this personal, handsome, but all I ever want from you is for you to march right over to my place, right this very minute mister, and fuck me until I can't even remember my middle name anymore." Needless to say, I said a polite "maybe next time" and moved on. I didn't raise a fuss because I was worried I'd get blackballed. I'd read an article once about some guy down in Hollywood named Harvey who would always make life miserable for any actress who would raise a stink with the studio. I knew if I wanted to make it to the top of my profession, I was going to have to take my lumps and keep my mouth shut. I'm glad I did because in a very short time, I'd landed two lucrative business architecture contracts: one with the Office of the Chief Information Officer for the Province of B.C., and the other with BC Ferries. Shortly thereafter I was elected by all my peers in business as President of the Institute of Certified Management Consultants of B.C. Soon I was helping to co-manage that proposed $49 million investment in modern IT infrastructure at BC Transit. Soon came a trip down to Fort Lauderdale to deliver a speech on business design excellence to a conference of corporate executives from all across the U.S.

This all led to me landing a huge turning-point contract with National Instruments of Austin, Texas. Things just snowballed from there. It was contract after contract, after contract, until my final retirement in 2019. What a crazy world we live in when newcomers have to sleep with predators in power just to make a go of it. What a world when a man with the mind and maturity of an 8-year-old—still beaming with pride over some diorama contest from 1966 at Balmoral Public School—can skate circles around the likes of Deloitte, IBM and KPMG. Indeed I was no E.P. Taylor, but I sure as hell knew how to find my way through the schoolyard of life.

When I finalized my mental health therapy sessions with Reilly I finally got around to telling her about that array of women with whom I got involved from 2000 to 2018. But before getting into the details I mentioned to her that in the 13 years when I was married to Marianne beforehand there were quite a number of women who also attempted to lead me astray, similar to what all those married women did in the early 1980s. I advised that although none of these interlopers had been successful in taking me away from Marianne, they were nonetheless very persuasive. Almost always they proposed something transactional. They would most often say, "I'm not a homewrecker, handsome, but this is just something I need." The word "something" usually meant wild erotic sex in exchange for a hot tip on some breaking news story. Television news reporters in the '90s were most persistent. If you're curious to know what these reporters were really like, then watch the film *Richard Jewell*—and pay close attention to the character played by Olivia Wilde. If you want to know what they looked like, then pay close attention to the character played by Olivia Wilde. If you want to understand why they would resort to such tactics, pay close attention to the character played by Olivia Wilde.

It got even more intense after *Vancouver* magazine published a full-page feature on all the local police spokespersons called Cop-Land. It described Constable Anne Drennan, Constable Elly Sawchuk, Constable Grant Learned and me as "celebrities" and me in particular as "cute" and a guy with "superior hair." Knowing I was male—and believing I was hopelessly weak—that one station across town thought they could wear me down with all their after-shift 'erect nipple' parties down at The Yale. But honestly, asking me if I'd ever seen groups of pencil skirt women making out with each other, in order to see whose nipples would go hard first, was like asking Gretzky if he'd ever seen a hockey puck. In fairness to Gretzky, no one ever insisted *Walk This Way* by Run-DMC be blaring in the background. When I served as the daily spokesperson for the on-duty shooting of Constable Laurie White in November of 1998, I later asked a high-profile television news reporter how she thought I did at the scrum I held just outside the emerg doors at VGH. She said, "Frankly, all I could think about was sex. I kept the B-roll in my purse so I could rub one off when I got home." She never asked how Laurie's amputation surgery went, or whether she was still in critical condition. I tried to feed her the exclusive that the Commissioner had denied use of an RCMP fixed wing—so Wally and Norah White could scramble out west just as quickly as possible to be at their wounded daughter's side— but she showed zero interest. She said the amount of voice over effort required wouldn't be worth the cost involved. She said the boys on the desk were already pissed off that too much airtime had been devoted two weeks ago to the death of Michel Trudeau. With no visuals of a frozen and contorted body to parade out, their A-block slot had been a total ratings flop. I guess when that award-winning journalist John Stossel had me interviewed in 1998 for that episode of ABC's 20-20 called *Sex, Drugs & Consenting Adults* he really had no frigging idea I had a lot more experience in these matters than simply speaking to the socially accepted recreational use of cannabis across Canada.

There were of course all those coworkers with whom Marianne worked at the Richmond Savings Credit Union and at Eaton's Lansdowne Mall. For them, it was less of a transactional thing and more a saucy vixen thing. For some reason wanting to be tied up and blindfolded by a rising star Mountie seemed to be the in-thing in the late 1980s. They weren't shy about letting Marianne know their intentions either. They often asked her if they could borrow me for the weekend. They would show up at the house offering to hang wallpaper and climb high ladders wearing only tube tops and micro-mini skirts. They would insist I hold the ladder steady so I could get a good look at their undercarriage. Heck, one even plunged her hands down my pants and grabbed my junk right in front of Marianne at a dinner party. They weren't wearing Buster Brown shoes, swinging skipping ropes, or chewing gum with pigtails, but they still sure as hell circled like sharks at the base of our driveways out in Steveston and over in Chilliwack. Even without a radio flyer wagon, they never missed an opportunity to ask Marianne if Russell could come out to play. They would always say, "Oh my, he's got such bedroom eyes. Does he have a twin brother who's single?" I had so many stalkers and hangers-on Marianne would often say to me at supper, "Hey, I saw your girlfriend today at Save-on-Foods, and oh ya, Nicki from the Lancôme counter says hi." As I always say to anyone who ever doubts the veracity of any of my disclosures about women over six decades, "Give me a minute and I'll tee-up that 1998 'I-want-to-grab-Russ-Grabb' video produced by several women at CBC. It pulls no punches in its lurid depiction of the man who was the most senior RCMP spokesperson for British Columbia in the late 1990s, who received no end of sexualized attention from no end of panting women." It was a cleverly edited romp—bridged with risqué voice overs—that was intended to gin up innocent levity and break tension at the CBC's ever struggling television studio over on Hamilton Street. It employed slow motion close-ups of arching females staring deep into my eyes and coveting my backside. It depicted what some of the producers working there claimed was happening to me all across town at all the other news outlets—without me even realizing it. One producer said friendly wagers were being taken everywhere as to which female reporter would be the first to wear me down and get me naked. It's all in the video that I still have safely stored on my laptop computer to this very day.

It was around this time that I think Reilly was really starting to question the prevailing literature on who really hunts who out there in this Darwinian world of primal sex and human struggle. You be your own judge, but I've always maintained there's a side of women nobody ever really wants to talk about. Anybody who ever tries just ends up eviscerated into oblivion. I saw it firsthand on December 28, 1960. The CBC amplified it with that video in 1998. It was Reilly who pointed out that aside from those five years in Guildwood Village in high school, I was just about everybody's disposable sexual ashtray every single day for close to 60 years. She was particularly irked learning about that naked psych major Maria who hounded me nonstop when I was helping to investigate the brutal murder of Kevin Ladouceur down on Wreck Beach in 1990. She almost lost her shit when she heard about some federal government executive in 2007 dangling the false promise of a $25,000 consulting contract if I'd only grant her one night of Kid Rock serenaded sex. She didn't even want to hear about that marathon running married couple in Victoria who, in 2011, said they could open some doors for me with some deep-pocket clients—if I'd only drop by for a little 'strictly heterosexual' exploration at their summer cabin. Once Reilly learned it was the 28-year-old wife who'd reached out to me first, she said, "Stop, I've heard enough!" It took my 2017 stroke, and the commensurate aging of my ever-youthful Norman Rockwell painting face, for me to no longer be a target of any of it. There would be no more Richard Gere and Abercrombie & Finch male model comparisons. No more being cat called the Silver Fox by twenty-something waitresses. Never again would some woman say, "Oh Russ, you're so pretty." Never again would three Etobicoke housewives pass little Gorgeous George around the kitchen table like a piece of sexualized meat. Aside from having Marianne and the girls back in my life, it was the best thing to ever happen to me. Who knew a massive near-death occlusion in the right middle cerebral artery of my brain would be the very thing that I needed to make it all finally go away? No coincidence the stroke itself was inextricably linked to alcohol abuse and a 1977 case of myocarditis—both triggered and set in motion by childhood trauma and sexual defilement inflicted upon me by guess who? The very female and all her later-in-life avatars about whom I'm not allowed to speak for fear of being pulverized into cancel-culture oblivion that's who. Stay tuned and you'll hear just exactly who all these Grabbatars as I call them actually were. They were the women who just couldn't stop singing "keep on lovin' me baby" as they plunged a bloodstained axe into my ever-weakened soul. They were the ones who would always spitball over light dinner conversation, "Oh ya, Jack Kennedy. Funny you should bring him up, Russ. He's so handsome. And so deliciously American too. If he were still alive, and if he still looked anything today like he did in 1960, I'd so fuck him in a heartbeat, if I ever had half the chance. Wouldn't you, Russ? If you were me?"

**CHAPTER 15:** The Language of Incest

AS I SET OUT to craft this memoir, I scoured the planet looking for that one defining-moment song whose stinging lyrics might capture the aching essence of my extraordinary life. Several songs stood out for me, but ultimately I landed on the 1971 hit, *Where Evil Grows* by The Poppy Family. Its probing lyrics betrayed what actually motivated me to fall so deeply in love so often with the wrong person after my separation from Marianne in 2000. It betrayed that my attraction to a certain type of woman was actually a lot less about them, and so much more about my own failings as a man. It betrayed that most of the evil that afflicted me so horrendously during this wine-drenched period was actually the pre-assigned proclivity for danger and dysfunction that had been flourishing deep inside of me the whole time. If you have a few moments, have a close listen to this song by The Poppy Family. It will go a long way to explaining the rather insane description of Darwinian depravity and sexual cannibalism that you're about to read. I'm not saying I'm the one who is irredeemably evil. As you'll soon learn, I'm merely pointing out that the unhappy events of Etobicoke, Drummondville, Bramalea and Scarborough forever condemned me to a life of inexcusable debauchery and poor judgement.

---

So the full report that I gave to Reilly on what I call The Disaster and my 2000-to-2018 quest to find everlasting love again was nothing short of a doozy. Some are saying it makes the screenplay for *Alfie* read like a tepid script for an episode of *Barney & Friends*. It broke down like this. Over the course of that fucked-up 18-year period I became romantically involved with an array of women from a wide range of demographic backgrounds. Most were just really nice people. All had very respectable jobs and educational backgrounds. All initially came across as adorable, loveable and kind. But some were unquestionably afflicted with visibly manifested personality disorders. Now I'm no clinician by any stretch, but through my extensive training and experience with homicide investigations, I certainly absorbed a lot of formalized reading on sub-clinical psychopathy and the human condition. Papers written by Dr. Bob Hare at UBC were particularly helpful. Meeting with that FBI behavioral scientist in 1988 to discuss the Green River serial killer case near Tacoma—and catch a briefing on the then brandnew ViCAP booklet then being circulated to law enforcement across the U.S.—was certainly an eyeopener for me. Dealing with forensic psychiatrist, Dr. Semrau, on the Dr. Tyhurst serial rape case in 1989 made a real lasting impression on me. During this 18-year period I believe I saw examples of narcissist personality disorders, at least one histrionic personality disorder, and possibly one case of high-functioning psychosis. Without question, there was at least one borderline personality disorder in the mix that most certainly mimicked all the psychopathy markers long observed in my mother back in the day. I say without question in this instance in part because the woman herself—a highly educated person—told me her therapist had long diagnosed her with this irreversible condition. Another women with whom I became involved broke down in tears late one night to confess she'd been several times diagnosed as a disordered narcissist who would be forever condemned to living a life replete with chaos and anguish—a life where she'd, by no fault of her own, oscillate from periods of tender affection and kindness, to searing anger and abject cruelty.

As I say, most of these women during this time were just really nice people who treated me with great kindness and affection. It was all the others for whom I strangely possessed an unstoppable schoolyard crush weakness. From them I derived a calming familiar embrace and the sense that it was my celestial divinatory calling to be there for them. I was forever breaking up with all the really nice women—and forever asking out the noticeably disordered ones.

As it relates to these troubled folks, there really wasn't much of that gentle intimacy that I'd set out to find. There was much walking around the house naked from the waist down. Most insisted that while having sex with me I tell them stories of how I once fucked another woman, and made her cum repeatedly like there was no tomorrow. The details about this other woman being powerless to resist my thrusts was their favourite part. Rather than finding untroubled peace, I often found myself embroiled in distressing conundrums where my romantic interest would binge on porn and talk filthy dirty in bed. With these disordered ones, I lost count how many times I had to endure the sound of them yelling, "Fuck me baby, fuck me please. Pound me baby, pound me harder. Take me, take me now." Most evenings I just wanted to cuddle and hold hands, but they seemed to have this rather red-hot fixation with cunniligus and screaming out obscenities in front of a mirror in the master bedroom—not dissimilar to what I heard from my mother way back in 1962 in Drummondville when I was 5.

From the really nice women I heard endless tales of a happy future where they'd all find lasting romance, and grow old with an irredeemably romantic chap like me. From the troubled ones, I heard no end of disquieting stories of prior abuse and abandonment. Many had been given up for adoption as an infant. One was raped when she was 6. Most had been incessantly sexually harassed and demeaned in the workplace. Strangely, many claimed that anal sex with a muscular hunk was their ultimate sexual fantasy. It was the notion of being taken that turned them on the most. It's pretty much all they talked about. One by one, most eventually disclosed without any prompting that their high interest in girl-on-girl sex and threesomes wasn't about being bi-curious. They said it was because men were just so God damn lame in the sack. Two of them even said that I was nothing more than boy bait to attract who they really wanted to be with. They said they hated men, but needed them to serve a purpose. It was not dissimilar to how personality disordered Karla Homolka saw my old neighbour and infamous serial killer, Paul Bernardo—except that none of the women I was with ever asked me to help her sedate, sexually desecrate, and murder her own 15-year-old sister on video tape. The sexually charged rooftop patio at Joes Fortes on Thurlow in Vancouver was the sort of place where much of this cringeworthy overshare would typically spew unabated. Chichi house parties at some insanely ornate mansion on the shores of Gonzales Beach in Victoria was the place where it would often boil over into tortured ponderings as to whether we should go with the debutante BCom from Royal Roads in the Burning Man frock or simply the gallery curator in Kate Spade from Tahoe.

Most interesting for me was the fact that a small core of the disordered ones were pros at projecting and gaslighting. They were the women who would always refer to themselves in the third person. They would never say, "I went to the mall yesterday," or "I watched a great episode of *Law & Order* last night." They would instead quip, "Hey babe, did you know [insert her name] went to Metro Town yesterday?" or "Hey shithead, you'll be very proud, [insert her name] watched a lame episode of your favourite show last night." Four had their own put-the-peanut-butter-on-the-counter illness. One would tell me to put the lettuce away in the fridge, but not in the crisper. Ten minutes later she would scream, "Russ, for fuck sakes, how many times do I have to tell you to put the lettuce in the crisper." After I would put it away in the crisper, she would scream, "Russ, for fuck sakes, how many times do I have to tell you to not put the lettuce in the crisper." This would go on for 20 minutes before she would throw a glass of prosecco in my face and storm out of the kitchen. Another would insist that—in the interest of good old fashioned chivalry—I hold open the car door for her. Ten minutes later she would scream, "Russ, I'm not a fucking cripple over here. I can get my own car door." The next time we went out somewhere she would scream, "Russ, for fuck sakes, aren't you going to get the door?" One even threatened to plunge a knife in my chest while I was sleeping if I couldn't instantly guess what her expectations were for how the stupid dishrag should be draped over the kitchen faucet. I let it happen all the time because I was irredeemably addicted to all their ebb-and-flow affection. I used to derive such a warm glow from all their oscillating depravity. I was heartened none of them ever expressed any interest in ordering from the Victoria's Secret catalogue, but it intrigued me that all of these disordered 'peanut butter' ladies kept saying "I hate you, please don't leave me" over and over. Because of my own baleful pathology to always fall head over heels in love with danger and dysfunction, I was oblivious to the reality that all this would cause such great harm to my daughters. It never occurred to me that Marianne was back in Ottawa, worried sick about my general welfare and my deteriorating mental health. No I wasn't a retired police superintendent who deserved the respect and admiration of the masses for all his noble service. No I wasn't a business consultant deserving of wide industry recognition. I was a fool. I was a drunk. I was a fucking idiot who deserved to get his pathetic loser ass kicked.

To be clear, none of these troubled folks ever woke up in the middle of the night pledging to exact great pain and suffering upon anyone. They were all merely broken souls who had absolutely no conscious awareness of their destructive pathology. They were simply doing their level best to find their way somewhere before it was too late. They too were trying to find their Grandpa Fred and come to terms with some unspeakable trauma from their tormented past. They too had lived through some wretched Brentwood Drive nightmare. I never shared this with Reilly, but clearly part of my attraction to these women was more than me trying to please and win the admiration of a familiar embrace. I subconsciously thought that if I could rescue them from all their inner agony, I might somehow undo all history and render my mother the loving person she'd been before she dragged me out into a snowstorm by my hair on December 28, 1960. I reasoned at my most primal level that by doing this I might just rescue myself. For those of you who've lived the crushing despair of opposite-sex incest as a child—as I have—you know that, for us, sex is never about erotic pleasure, or seeking the brag badge of anything. For us, sex is always just language. You know, a lonely aching primordial language that allows us to revisit the place where it all started—all in the beguiled hope we might confront whoever did this to us. As Madonna would say, "It's just strangers making the most of the dark." It of course never works. Tragically, it just leads to more danger, more dysfunction. And while everyone of these troubled women was 'girl interrupted' just like my mother, I was undeniably—from every conceivable perspective—'boy broken' on a mission to cut a swath and self-destruct.

As I bring these revelations about all my later-in-life interactions with women to a close, I'm hopeful there'll be at least one reader out there in the universe who will get past the burning temptation to say, "OMG, what a douche bag that Russ Grabb guy was." I'm hoping at least one of you will see that a little boy who is forced by unchecked psychopathy into opposite-sex incest slavery as a child never really ends up living the kind of life that you ever imagined for yourself. Maybe you will also be that person who's already long deduced that I actually solved that Vegh cold case murder back in 1993, not because of some gumshoe crystal ball, or because Mr. McConnell said I was near-Mensa, but because I just happened to know a thing or two about opposite-sex incest—and how it changes everything both inside a family home and inside a human survivor.

I only wish I'd been a stronger child. I only wish I hadn't been so timid when I was little. I only wish I'd somehow found the strength to fend off all that terrible madness. I only wish I hadn't been such a raving asshole as an adult. My challenge now, no sorry, correction, my gift now will be to take all that I've endured, all that I've learned, and go be a better person, a better man, a better dad, a better husband, and a decent human who will share acquired insight with the universe instead of fighting against it all the time. It's time to stop making the whole world pay for what just one person did, so very long ago. Encased in a punishing blanket of leukemia and cardiomyopathy, it's not going to be easy. It will, however, remain my undying obligation to those I love to make it so. After all the inexcusable heartache I've caused Marianne, Megan, and Alena—especially you Alena—I'd be a complete pompous jackass like what's-his-name to not make it my absolute *raison d'être* focus before it's truly my time to go to heaven.

# CHAPTER 16: Tucked in Our Struggles

I'M NOT SURE WHY, but when I follow the trail of breadcrumbs all the way back from where I am today with my life—free of self-imposed bitterness and ready to take my place in heaven—I'm always taken back to a specific turning point event which quite frankly I haven't given much thought to for over 30 years. It was yet another one those 92 murder cases within which I'd been asked to play some sort of tangential or mission critical role. It's weird because despite all my puerile attempts over the years to shamelessly brand myself as the mother of all major crime investigators, being in the RCMP was never really my identity. It was always just my job. In this current breadcrumb tracing exercise, I'm always taken back to April 8, 1989. It was a bright sunny day, and I was at the height of my Miami Vice constructed reality delusion. Dressed in Armani and shoed in Stefano Ricci, I was acting grumpy because I was right in the middle of writing an elaborate affidavit to obtain an array of wiretaps on yet another gang of murderous tweakers operating in the Vancouver region— and as luck would have it—my bloody pager went off. It was summoning me to lend a hand at the scene of a shallow grave and some skeletal remains found by a senior citizen walking her dog out near UBC in Pacific Spirit Park. Halfway through my glorious four year stint at "E" Division Serious Crime Section, I was pretty much certain I had better things to do. Mr. Justice Patrick Dohm was a real stickler for affidavit details, so it was vital that I not miss a single pen stroke with all my elegant loquacious prose.

So when I arrived on scene I noticed both the usual grid search underway in the surrounding forest and a bunch of white coat forensic specialists gathered tightly around the tiny pit within which was a decomposed cadaver consisting mostly of sun-bleached bones, rotting sinew, and long flowing head hair. The sight of maggots shimmering in unison was most unnerving. The smell was truly unbearable. A tiny fractured hyoid bone had already suggested homicidal death by strangulation. There was a lot to take in, and so many detailed notes to make. But mostly I noticed an elitist hierarchy of asserted competency and pious credentials all made possible by the tacit non-verbal communication of who you were in life, what school you had gone to, and what uppercase letters you had embossed after your name on your stupid business card. The ranking forensic pathologist was of course the mighty oracle at the scene whose eminence and insights were not to be questioned. He was the high priest of the exercise in front of whom we were all to obediently bow. Next in line was the local forensic odontologist. Although primarily focused on the examination of dental remains, his real job was to bellow "I concur" every time the ranking forensic pathologist uttered a pronouncement. Next came the two or three forensic identification technicians from the RCMP who frankly were only really there to take pictures of the elaborate ballet of forensic investigation incompetence, and create the grand illusion for the television cameras that admissible evidence was actually being collected at the scene. Boss man was the uniformed staff-sergeant in charge of the local University RCMP Detachment. He once saw a dead body on an episode of *Quincy* back in the '70s so he was perfectly qualified to assume tactical command. If he were lucky, a lowly sergeant or corporal from the "E" Division Serious Crime Section would also be invited over from the kids table to kibitz with the grown-ups. As a seasoned constable with extensive homicide investigation experience, I mattered not. It went without saying that I was to stand off to the side, keep very quiet, and let the big boys take it from here. Most were just expecting me to look pretty and help string do-not-cross tape between a bunch of pine trees. It was for no real discernible investigative purpose other than to perhaps amuse intrepid crime reporters like George Garrett, John Daly and Salim Jiwa.

Anyway, that's just what I noticed.

It was 1989 so police agencies and forensic pathologists across Canada did not yet have access to DNA forensics. With this body being found with no identification, no clothes, and no flesh left to fingerprint, the only way it was ever going to be identified was either through dental record comparison, or the matching of a distinctive bone trait to some pre-existing X-ray film. With there being so much advanced decomposition, determination of age and gender-at-birth was also going to be difficult. Laypersons who watch all those forensic investigation shows on TV would argue that comparisons of hairs and fibers would be helpful, but as an actual non-TV-watching homicide investigator I knew that was total hogwash. I knew that a couple of the wrongfully convicted across Canada were then currently rotting in prison because some nob at the lab had actually claimed to have made a positive hair or trace fiber match, when in fact no such comparison is ever scientifically possible.

As time passed the moment we had all been waiting for finally arrived. The great exalted forensic pathologist was ready to make his rarefied pronouncement. He held a large section of the shattered skull up to the sun and squinted with theatrical reflection. Strands of human hair clung to the plate like a terrified child with his arms wrapped tightly around his mother's ankle. Longer strands danced in the breeze and gave off the most horrific smell. Finally he announced with his manufactured Jeremy Irons accent, "Judging by the weathered texture and relational metrics of the cranium—and the presence of advanced ossification—I'd say caucasian male in his mid-to-late fifties." Right on script the nob forensic odontologist said, "I concur." Speaking completely out of turn, I blurted out, "Judging by the long blond hair and the French manicure toenails, I'd say 25-year-old female prostitute missing from the Downtown Eastside."

It's just what I noticed.

The collective fury of silence was palpable. There were icy stares all around. All the older RCMP members were noticeably vexed at my rank intransigence. The forensic pathologist was beside himself with silent outrage. The uniformed staff-sergeant in charge of everything gave me a stern look and a set of folded arms that was clearly intended to say, "You can go now."

True story. You just can't make this shit up.

This whole episode ended with me quietly heading over to see Detective Rick Crook at VPD, asking him if he could please fish out the dental chart records for a young woman who I knew had been missing from the Mount Pleasant area for about 6 months. I had a hunch these skeletal remains might be those of a woman by the name of Tracey Leigh Chartrand. Her name had come up in a briefing 4 months earlier on missing and murdered women in the Vancouver area. Unlike a certain media relations officer who had been suggesting that missing prostitutes were likely over in Calgary, or down in Seattle, studying to become office receptionists, I paid close attention to all the details. There was just something in Tracey's hair colour and style that stuck out in my mind. I'd never been to forensic pathology school—heck, I didn't even have a university degree—but I was smart enough to know that it's still very much possible for a 25-year-old woman from the hideous Downtown Eastside who's been raped, beaten, tortured and malnourished since birth to have just as many stress-induced ossifications on her skull as any whiny bitch white-privilege male from the burbs in his mid-to-late fifties. One gets real old real fast when one is enslaved in a pit of normalized desecration and perpetual violence just a few blocks away from Holt Renfrew and the Provincial Cabinet boardroom over at Canada Place.

It was a selfless act on my part without which Tracey would have never been identified and repatriated back to her loving family. Within two days of me being escorted off the crime scene, the local coroner had formalized the positive identification of Tracey Leigh Chartrand, age 25, of no fixed address. He did so based solely on the dental records that I'd received from Detective Crook. To this day, her murder remains unsolved, but without me having exercised the courage to once again spit squarely in the face of Canadian meritocracy, her remains would have been dumped into a cardboard box with a shovel and stored forever on some barren shelf at some prosaic coroner's office over on Keefer Street. She would have been catalogued in some heartless handwritten ledger as just some John Doe decedent from who knows where.

It was a turning point moment that prompted me to notice that things aren't always as they seem in this crazy fucked-up world.

It was an episode in my life that reminded me of that earlier time when my good friend Dr. Raymond Corrado from SFU invited me over to stay with him and his family for two weeks when he was then serving as a Visiting Fellow at Cambridge University. It was December 1985. It was just three weeks before I would finally work up the courage to ask Marianne out on our very first date, and woo her with six live lobsters and a bottle of Dom at the cozy little house in Whistler that she then co-owned with her sister, Sue.

Raymond was older than me, and oddly enough, he was my main night school professor at SFU. We became close friends because we were like-minded on so many subjects. We were suckers for the company of anyone with half a brain. As we grew closer in the 1980s, he roped me in to delivering tri-yearly lectures in one of his 2nd-year criminology courses. He once said he felt like Professor Lambeau from *Good Will Hunting*, in that he plucked me from obscurity because I maintained a 4.2 GPA in his program even though I spent all my time cutting class and badmouthing the rampant intellectual laziness of the human race. It was just so much fun being able to get up in front of 200 eager students and cut loose with my George Carlin sarcasm humour and my caustic Bill Maher social-justice commentary lens, as I mercilessly carved up the trappings of sanctimonious Canadian culture and all the delusions that we harbour about crime and punishment. It's so funny how a man himself encased in so much ill-gotten delusion could be so clever at spotting even greater delusion in the actions and belief systems of others.

Takes one to know one, I guess.

When Raymond invited me to join him for lunch one afternoon at some faculty club at Cambridge, I was taken aback by the lack of elevated intellect being exhibited by all the exalted academics in attendance. Here I was dining at the very table where Sir Isaac Newton no doubt sat as a cash-strapped mathlete, back in 1669, and all the professors around me seemed, well, you know, unusually stupid and grossly misinformed. I had heard intellectual exchanges and clever banter far more superior to this between a bunch of high school grad Mounties at Bino's Family Restaurant up on Lonsdale at 4:37 a.m. in North Vancouver. The posse from City North were particularly astute. City South and Capilano less so, but you get my drift. Raymond was clearly a genius, but all these mucky mucks from Cambridge seemed, well, you know, dumber than day-old hamsters. It was yet another moment when I had to accept the fact there was no Santa, no Easter Bunny and no Tooth Fairy. Elitism and grandeur were just brandings shallow people cook up in order to inflict their poorly reasoned will upon the innocent. Whether it's a noble scholar from Cambridge, a forensic pathologist, the Commissioner of the RCMP, or just some assistant deputy minister over in Victoria masquerading as an executive leader, modern society had become infested with great pretenders who think they can get away with just about anything. They fake it until they make it. It's never about those who actually matter. It's always just about them, their lofty credentials, their silly tools, and their idolized disciplines of study.

It would take someone with my embattled history to ever really notice such things. As I found out firsthand over the course of 60 some odd years, it would always take the use of hand puppets and crayons—and the avoidance of sentences longer than five words—to ever get these great exalted ones to ever pay attention to even the simplest of universal truths. Having to reconsider their obsession with perfected process, and go focus on the noble outcome instead was simply beyond their reach. I mean where was the TED Talk glory in that? You could never get them to see that it's actually being abandoned, ignored, and devalued—and not organizational change—that humans fear.

When I was investigating a fresh homicide case out in Chilliwack in 1991 it occurred to me that the best way to find out who stabbed this young heroin addict sitting on the couch at that rancid shooting gallery downtown would be to go visit his buddies down the street at that other shithole where they usually went for breakfast after a night of partying, chipping China White, and breaking into parked Honda Civics. Upon my arrival there I sensed that this was a different crowd today. They seemed less hostile and more likely to be talkative. One woman in particular appeared to be giving me blinking-eye signals similar to all those POWs who send morse code messages back to their loved ones in the States that they're being tortured by their North Vietnamese captors. I figured the best way to solve this murder would be to crack a few jokes and get the fuck out of there just as soon as possible. I saw a bunch of broken souls who just seemed really exhausted with the whole degrading drug addiction lifestyle.

It would take someone with a similarly broken soul to ever really care.

When I got back to the detachment office later that morning the woman who had been sending me those morse code messages telephoned me confidentially to tell me who the killer was, where the knife could be found, and where to go make the arrest. A couple hours later the killer was arrested by a member of our team as he was trying to board a boat to Victoria at the Tsawwassen ferry terminal. We had the case all wrapped up by supper time. Two years later I asked that woman why she had been so cooperative, at great risk to her own personal safety. She wasn't the only determinant in solving this case, but she was certainly significant. She said it was because I had reminded her of her grandpa when I cracked all those corny dad jokes. She said me making reference to Sting singing in the background, and how that was just such a curious link to The Police being present at their house, at that very moment, was a real knee-slapper. She said how I handled things with such quiet regal grace and authentic compassion just made her feel like she should pay it forward. It's just how we solved crime back in the day.

In August of 2001, when I was wrapping up my two year secondment to DND, the then Vice Chief of Defence Staff called me into his office to ask me what I—as a detective investigator from the RCMP—had learned from my short stay with the Canadian Armed Forces. Sensing he was looking for a full-throated answer, I told him that what I'd seen was an element of the senior chain of command—pig men at the rank of Major and above—who possessed a perverse sense of entitlement and a cavalier disregard for the greater good. Bewildered and unable to reply, he just sat motionless. I concluded by saying, "Anyway that's just what I noticed. Take it for what it's worth. You're the Admiral, I'm the Inspector. What the hell would I really know?"

In the early summer of 2010, when I was on my way over to Paris with Megan and Alena to celebrate Alena's survival 8 months earlier from TSS, I was delighted to see my Helijet chit-chat buddy—Provincial MLA Jenny Kwan—onboard our flight with her husband and children. Almost immediately I noticed she was not her normal friendly self. She did reluctantly spit out that they were on their way over to Vienna, but she did everything she could to avoid saying anything further. Almost immediately my instincts started firing off smelly cheese alarm bells. I thought nothing further of it until four years later when she held a presser to apologize for the shameful misuse of public funds by her husband to cover a family vacation to Europe. For me, it was the fact these funds were supposed to have been allocated to providing homes for impoverished Indigenous peoples in the Downtown Eastside that really fried my ass.

So ya, I guess being that contrarian fellow who always noticed things that everyone else seemed to miss was indeed what defined me as a person as I progressed through my adulthood. As you can see, it came in real handy working on all those high-profile major crime cases. It of course paid huge dividends when, as a senior executive with the RCMP, I was asked to rescue and get back on track all those organizational leadership and program design fiascos. I guess it's why all those lawyers kept telling me to quit the RCMP and go get a law degree. As I was retiring from the workforce in 2019, one of the dissenters on my business consulting team said that if there was any truth to what I claim to notice about digital-tech software then Boeing airliners would simply fallout of the sky. I replied, "You mean like last week in Ethiopia, or the year before in Indonesia?" A year after I won that hefty contract with National Instruments of Texas I asked my client why—of all the folks he could have hired at that business innovation conference down in Florida—he picked little-old me. He said it was because when I delivered my keynote address in November of 2011, I reminded him of Andy Andrews, the author of that bestselling novel, *The Noticer*. I really wasn't sure what he meant by this, so I went off and did a little library research. Turns out the book was about this simple drifter guy who—despite not being highly educated or ordained with lofty credentials—had this rather unique gift of always being able to see what others couldn't. The thrust of the book was that it only takes a thoughtful understanding of people to recognize the miracles in our moments, and the seeds of greatness tucked in our struggles. It was an allegory piece that suggested that it had been the drifter's life of hardship—and not anything venerated, revered or iconic—that bestowed him with such a wonderful gift. It was the notion that if you don't notice what's really going on, if you don't get the fix right the first time then, well, people die, children suffer, whole communities decay, and hope evaporates from the collective soul of the very people you've committed to serve.

Anyway, it's just what I always notice. I'm never going to be just some sleep-deprived straphanger on the bus to adulated elitism. Grandeur worship is what set the grand pristine stage to rob me of my childhood back in the 1960s. It's what almost got me murdered by you-know-who.

# CHAPTER 17: Stark Reflections

I KNOW WHAT YOU'RE THINKING. You understand that this is the aching diary of a man who suffered the unspeakable when he was a child, who later went on to live a life of great torment as an adult. You found what he had to say about his encounters with women to be off-putting and overwrought, but you get it and you wish there's something you could do to assist. On the other hand, you're Canadian so you just can't help yourself, can you? You want to hear more. But not more about his suffering and his quiet quest for healing. You want to hear more about homicide cases—and all his salacious encounters with gangsters and the many persons of prominence into whom he often bumps just going about his regular man existence. I'm sorry to break it to you Pumpkin, but the most shocking 'noticer' episode I could ever share isn't about yet-another murder case. It isn't about some sanctimonious act of elitism being imposed upon the unsuspecting by the undeserving. It's not about some celebrity tearing up at an Earl's. You see, when I looked in the mirror one morning in 2013, I noticed what was clearly the beginning of my long expected end. It was that look of vacant hope that I'd seen so many times before in others. I was 56 years old and there was just something there that just didn't seem quite right. At first I thought it might be my addiction to medical merlot as a form of self-medication. Then I wondered if it might be all my debauchery down in Las Vegas. I mean listening to Paris Hilton one table over at the Mandarin yell "Utah, Utah, Utah" every seven seconds for two hours was enough to make any lost soul go have half snaky. Although I was in a perpetual state of denial myself, I just couldn't deny that I was then drinking well over two bottles of wine every night. Was it all the grief I'd been causing Alena? Was it because I so very much missed Marianne? Perhaps it was because of the big lies I kept telling myself in order to keep all my constructed realities afloat? Then boom. Just like that I noticed what it really was. I noticed that the broken nose that had been following me around since 1965 was finally starting to decay. It was starting to collapse right before my very eyes. I had been told multiple times by clinicians over the years to go get it repaired, but I kinda liked having a weathered face that made me look like Mickey Rourke from the film, *9½ Weeks*. I thought it sort of went well with what all the ladies would say were my chocolate brown eyes. I was also worried that getting it fixed might inch me closer to having to toss aside all my scurrilous delusions and go face the reality that as a child I had been grotesquely beaten, sexually defiled, and gaslit into a perpetual state of delirium by my very own mother. One gets real old real fast when one is dragged right back to those enchanting places of institutionalized enslavement and moist Sara Lee coffee cake served on Grandma's fine china.

So, when I went to see prominent plastic surgeon Dr. Ken Smith of Victoria in 2014—to inquire what I might be able to do about my nose—he asked if I'd ever fallen on my face from a three story building. He questioned whether I'd ever been a cocaine addict. He said that as a practitioner who often performs rhinoplasties on retired NHL players, he'd never before seen a septum so badly decimated. When I told him my full childhood history he immediately leapt into action. He was like Batman going after the fucking Riddler. He performed two major facial reconstruction surgeries spread 18 months apart; the second more tricky one of which involved the harvesting of a large chunk of rib material from my right torso in order to craft a new bridge for my nose. He wrote a rather kind letter that I was able to pass along to the Canada Revenue Agency so I could claim his fee as a legitimate medical expense. His letter said, "Russ required reconstructive surgery of his nose secondary to trauma which occurred in his youth. He has a known history of childhood trauma. He may require further interventions." Because there was a notion of esthetics involved in both surgeries, this wasn't something that was covered by my public healthcare plan. Before each surgery all the cardio diagnostics showed a preexisting left ventricular hypertrophy, or LVH, which was a downstream outfall of my myocarditis from 1977. There was however no sign of atrial fibrillation or any other heart failure condition. I was finally released from Dr. Smith's first-rate care and follow-up monitoring in the spring of 2016.

Now whereas you might think that getting such profound closure on my horribly broken beak would have prompted me to rebound with great optimism and psychiatric recuperation, it couldn't have been any further from the truth. The combination of alcoholism and repressed memory flashbacks—together with all the depression side effects from two prolonged general anesthetic procedures—just made matters worse. By the fall of 2016, all those terrible suicidal ideations from high school and Ryerson in the late 1970s were once again percolating to the surface. Every time I boarded Helijet I prayed it would nosedive into an unsurvivable fireball over on Saturna Island. I prayed every day the Grim Reaper would swoop in and take me away. I just couldn't wait to die. All the mounting shame and searing despair was simply unbearable.

On January 5, 2017, when I was walking home from a meeting in downtown Victoria, I almost got my wish. As I placed all my weight on my left foot, a giant clot broke loose from my heart and landed right in the right middle cerebral artery of my brain. Instantly blind and left-side hemiplegic, I lost my balance and flipped upside down right in front of an oncoming BMW. Somehow I managed to avoid being run over. Somehow I avoided being rendered permanently brain damaged. Somehow I evaded sudden death. I spent 10 days in Victoria General Hospital telling my remarkable story of stroke recovery to a small army of bewildered neurologists. They were all wondering how it was that I now had a raging case of atrial fibrillation; something that wasn't present when I had my two rhinoplasties not long before. I lied and made zero mention of intensified wine consumption, terrifying night-sweat dreams, and the reoccurring sensation of drowning in shallow tap water while pales of human excrement coiled up in my underpants.

———————————⟶

When Marianne and I started dating in early 1986—right after my crazy fucked-up visit to Cambridge University—we were both in our late twenties, so of course we conjured up this perfectly harmless fantasy that we were the indisputable power couple of Whistler. She lived up there in a house in Whistler Cay Heights, and I lived down in Richmond in a quaint seaside townhouse where married women who loved their husbands were known to crawl half-naked through open bedroom windows. There was some distance between us, but somehow we found a way to make it work. I would drive up to the village on my days off, and she would pop down to the city on hers. Although not rich and famous like all the Heathens of Howe Street, we were constantly in the company of all the top chefs and club owners. They even had enthralling European names like Pascal, Jean-Jacques, Joel and Simone. We of course never missed a chance to dine at Umberto's and knock back gallons of Dom Perignon. It was pretty cool that one night when the entire Toshiba family from Japan sat at the table right next to us. Seeing all those toddlers and little girls wearing all those tiny mink coats to match their mother was a sight to be seen. Always adorned with big hair and wide-shoulder jackets, we were of course heavy into dance music. Sure Madonna and Van Halen were all the rage, but for us it had to be hardcore '80s or nothing. We were constantly blasting *I'll Melt With You* by Modern English, *Send Me an Angel* by Real Life, *West End Girls* by the Pet Shop Boys, and *One Thing Leads to Another* by The Fixx. We were always there twice a week when Club 10 would close down at 2:00 a.m. and play *New York, New York* by Frank Sinatra. As Depeche Mode would say, "Just can't get enough." Heck, there was even that time when a sultry young woman in her early twenties joined us on the dance floor. When all the music stopped she tried to kiss Marianne, asking if we could both please just take her home for the night. I gave Marianne that look of 'I'm down with this if you are?' Marianne snapped, "This isn't going to happen, let's go, get your fucking coat." It wasn't long there after that Marianne and I got married and had two pig-tail pretty daughters down in Lotus Land. The rest as they say is history. *Crazy for You* by Madonna was the slow song at our wedding. It was Marianne's way of signaling that she'd never try to murder me in my sleep, but she'd do her best to keep me happy. Never in the history of humanity would there ever be a more touching tale of true love and devotion to fragile innocence shared with the universe. My long lamented earth angel had finally arrived. Only I could screw it all up now, right? I was of course oblivious to the reality that the Reverend who married us in that cute little chapel at the base of Whistler Mountain was the mother of that young lady Tammy who died of a drug overdose—but not before she married the slimiest Heathen of Howe Street of them all: a creepy lowlife geezer named Murray Pezim who was that always-on-the-fleece owner of the BC Lions.

With all the many health issues that had been building up with me in 2017—alcoholism, stroke, facial reconstruction, atrial fibrillation, and oh ya, depression—my mindset started to shift big time. The passage of time in the neurosciences ward gave me a chance to quietly reflect on where I was going with my life. I started to shift from sick suicidal ideations to the practical realities of survival. The big breakthrough came when Alena came to see me in the ICU the day after my stroke and told me it was her turn to hold my hand and tell me it was going to be okay. She reminded me of those times when she was little, when she would always nap on my chest on Sunday afternoons as I laid on the couch watching NFL football, referring to her as Snoopy, and me as the big lazy Doghouse. As Alena crawled in beside me she said, "I'm here now, Dad. You're the Snoopy now." She gave me a big hug and told me how very much I would always be loved. Megan did likewise. Marianne had moved back to Vancouver four months earlier—and was now living unpartnered with Megan—but I had yet to completely extricate myself from an ongoing relationship, so it would have been awkward if she too had been there. I sure wouldn't have minded though. I could have sworn I could smell her Estée Lauder perfume from Whistler on Megan's sweater sleeve. I know it may sound over-the-top cheesy, but I'm pretty sure I had that song *Send Me an Angel* stuck in my head the whole bloody time I was in the ICU.

Within six months of my release from hospital after my stroke I had made a full recovery and was well on my way to getting all my affairs in order. I was soon no longer in a relationship. I was soon moving forward with making substantive plans for the future. Being 60 years old, I figured I had another 38 years of good living left. I had every confidence my heart health would improve on its own, and that with some good old fashioned luck I would turn the corner on all my many mental health challenges, perhaps even cut way back on all the red wine. Strangely enough, this was also the period when my consulting firm really started to take off. Between a couple of local technology companies and multiple government ministries, I just continued to land contract after contract. Our team grew to 20 full and part-time associates, some of whom included three former assistant deputy ministers, two former CIOs, one former IBM partner, and a marketing instructor from Royal Roads. Things were going so well I started looking into commercial properties that I might lease to create what my team joked ought to be called the global world headquarters of Russ Grabb & Associates Inc. We were the only consulting firm in B.C. who gave out M&M chocolates embossed with our snappy teal-coloured corporate logo. But at no time did anyone twig to the fact that the colour teal had a much broader meaning for me. I guess nobody ever bothered to Google the phrase "official colour of sexual assault awareness."

On September 1, 2017, I finally made the call. It was the call I'd been dying to make for 18 years. Yup, I finally just up and called Marianne. I told her I'd been thinking at lot about her lately, and with her having moved back to Vancouver from Ottawa, it was perhaps time for the two of us to consider some sort of reconciliation. To my great surprise and joy she said she had been waiting for this call for 18 years, that she'd been dying inside as a person, and that she'd very much like to explore what ever options might still be possible after all this time. She told me how very much she still loved me and how she'd spent endless nights in Ottawa with a box of wine and a Blue Rodeo CD crying her bloody eyes out. We spoke for hours on the phone and agreed to give it a try, but to go slow and not rush in. We very much wanted this to last forever.

It was a good thing that Marianne was ready to talk about reconciliation because by the end of September 2017 my cardiologist was calling to report that a recent diagnostic had found a distressing aneurism in my right wrist. It was the nasty consequence of an earlier angiogram that didn't go so well. I was scheduled for an urgent surgery to have it extracted right away. If it broke loose it would surely disfigure my right hand, or worse, race straight up to my lungs and kill me dead with a massive pulmonary embolism. Recent diagnostics had also shown the ejection fraction of my heart had plunged to 40 percent. With my resting heart rate dipping to 42 beats per minute—and with my atrial fibrillation pounding away unabated—I was close to contracting the kind of cardiomyopathy condition that killed George Michael the year before.

Although my aneurism surgery went fairly well without too many complications, it was not without its scary moments. Unable to undergo yet another general anesthetic procedure, I was kept awake the whole time with an IV drip of fentanyl and ativan. It was so gross thinking of that pea-sized clot being cut out with a scalpel while some squiggly worm-like slice of vein further up the arm was harvested and grafted back into the hole in the wrist. Between the rib tissue in my nose and the borrowed vein in my wrist, science was busy scrounging spare parts from one part of my body in order to stop another from failing. When I got home my arm was so purple and grotesquely swollen it looked like it'd just been caught in a combine harvester. Although Marianne was still living over in Vancouver with Megan, she was there at my side the whole time. She even stayed for a few days at my place in Victoria and cooked me a special Thanksgiving turkey dinner. She was no doubt practicing for what was to come next. Little did either of us know, this was just the beginning of my downward health spiral. We gleefully spent the next eight months carefully planning our trial reconciliation. It culminated with her finally moving in with me in Victoria on May 23, 2018. It was so much fun watching my dog Lupin bounce up and down with so much gusto. It was the first time I'd seen Lupin not run and hide in the bathtub behind the shower curtain whenever some love interest came bounding through the front door. We both knew we'd made some big mistakes along the way—and were perhaps undeserving of such a blissful second chance—but we just knew it was nothing short of a true blessing. It would take an all-out nuclear war with the dirty Commies and an asteroid strike to ever tear us apart again. Marianne was ready for battle. God help any fuck stick Grabbatar who ever again tried to climb that wallpapering ladder, or crawl through that open fucking window.

~~~~~~

It's hard to believe, but by the fall of 2018—right after Marianne moved in with me—I had to have yet another emergency surgery. This time it is was to cut away a grapefruit-sized hydrocele cyst from my right testicle. It was a gory procedure that landed me right back in the ER the very next day when my 28 testicle stitches split wide open and my bladder went straight into a state of arrested flow. I had to have 1.6 litres of urine pumped from my bladder before it burst. I had to wear a catheter at home for two weeks before my bladder finally started working again on its own. Poor Marianne was stuck having to clean up all my spills and empty my bag, sometimes three or four times in the middle of the night. Poor Lupin had to watch us scurry about like a couple of drunk toddlers chasing a slippery beach ball over at the local playground. The pain in the man zone was worse than anything ISIS could ever inflict upon an imprisoned infidel with a pair of rusty pliers while they have him chained to a backyard fence in Etobicoke, I mean Mosul. I was doing my best to break free of negative ruminations, but a part of me just couldn't help but think this was probably the Goddesses of Fate making me pay for all my many transgressions. As it turned out, it wasn't just my pulverized nose that I'd noticed in the mirror back in 2013. Turns out, I was looking at an entire body that had been decimated beyond any measure by you know who—and all her rank depravity. Turns out, this was just the beginning of what would soon become the most agonizing time of my entire life. Stark reflections indeed. I didn't need a manufactured Jeremy Irons accent to understand I was in big fucking trouble.

# CHAPTER 18: Saved by Zero

I'VE LEARNED firsthand over the past few years that all journeys of leukemia cancer invariably begin with the phrase, "Oh, it's probably nothing." I know this not just from personal experience, and all the agony that goes with it, but also from chatting with other patients at the leukemia and bone marrow transplant clinic over at VGH. I also saw it in the retelling of every single child leukemia story ever posted on YouTube by frightened parents all across the world. Although leukemia most often ravages your body with a barrage of debilitating symptoms, it's not something that ever presents on an imaging device or through a biopsy as a tumour. The malignancies that drive this cancer exist only at the cellular level. You can't use a scalpel to cut out trillions of tiny malignant blood cells. You can't use radiation to target the source unless you want to place the patient in some sort of giant microwave oven and irradiate them to death. It's also hard to diagnose because its onset symptoms very often mimic harmless illnesses. It can only be treated with chemotherapy or bone marrow transplants. In rare cases, white blood immunities can be extracted from the patient and weaponized in the lab to be reintroduced to attack what are essentially 'malignant sister' blood cells. My rare type of incurable leukemia is one of the few that doesn't cause your lymph glands to swell. It also doesn't cause high spikes in lymphocytes either. You basically have to be at death's door with a complete immune system collapse and an exploding spleen before you qualify for a bone marrow biopsy and first line chemotherapy. In my case, it all started with me complaining about being anemic all the time. I of course got the languid "Oh, it's probably nothing, Mr. Grabb" response from all the experts. With 78 percent of my bone marrow having already turned to cancerous B-cell guacamole, an emergency department doctor who was treating me for fainting spells and severe nausea told me to "stop symptom shopping and just go home and have a nice warm bath."

Looking back now I realize that I'd gone from gazing in the mirror in 2013 and noticing the near-certain collapse of my broken nose, to undergoing two facial reconstruction surgeries, to experiencing a massive stroke and the onset of atrial fibrillation, and finally, to undergoing two more emergency surgeries: one to excise an aneurysm in 2017, and one to cut away a giant cyst from my testicle in 2018. All of these things were of course just cover for what was really going on with me. Behind all this was alcoholism, a progressive decline in my mental health, and an ever-deepening plunge in the ejection fraction score of my diseased heart. While friends and family continued to express well wishes for all these surgical interventions, Marianne and I knew what was really going on. We knew it was the unimaginable finally catching up with the unavoidable. The days of me being able to weave constructed realities as a crafty tool to survive paralyzing shame and despair were over. There would be no more compartmentalization. No more looking to partner with women who on a sub-conscious level reminded me of my mother. No more alcohol. Most of all, there would be no more Brioni suits and misguided crusades to follow through with that silly notion of a global world headquarters for some nascent business consulting company. Being that highly polished and much respected business consultant with a penchant for always landing big contracts with self-effacing humour and clever insights may have been seen by others as the mark of remarkable success, but it was never really who I was as a person. Just like the path that I'd taken years earlier with the RCMP, there wasn't a single monkey bar or swing set anywhere in the picture. There weren't any apple trees to climb either. Turns out owning the podium and grabbing the brass ring in every vocation into which I would randomly stumble wasn't anything I ever really wanted to do. Turns out being that autodidactic maverick with an enlarged caudate nucleus of the brain was just one giant curse. It prevented me from ever becoming who I really wanted to become: you know, that ordinary Joe man with a simple life and a modest passing interest in artistic expression and classical philosophy. This didn't mean that I was suffering from what all those pious experts would say was imposter syndrome. Imposter syndrome is when you think you've achieved great success that you don't actually deserve. For me it wasn't that I felt I didn't deserve any of my success in business—or earlier in the RCMP. For me it was that I never sought to achieve it in the first place. For me it was a matter that I never really got to be who I really was as a person. That quivering little tyke from Bramalea had every single fiber of hope and inspiration beaten out of him long before he even had any chance to get going with his adult life. Being the ever benevolent earth angel that she was, Marianne was going to change all that pronto. Now back in my life in 2018, she moved in with me over in Victoria and got to work immediately taking me under her wings. The first order of business would be to wind down all my company operations, sell the condo, and move back to Vancouver where we could be closer to Megan and Alena. Next up would be looking into the possibility of putting me in touch with an exceptional therapist who could finally help me find the inner peace and acceptance of self that I had been seeking for 62 years. I of course had in mind some fried pork chops with cream of mushroom soup sauce and minute rice—and a quiet evening at home on the couch with a little Bob Seger and Pink Floyd. I of course had in mind the purchase of a modest apartment over in Lower Lonsdale. With any luck, there might even be baked lasagna with some pipefitter welders down at the rickety old pier. With any luck I would return to those soothing moments of 1978 when I was able to set the pace and tempo of my very own life, free of imposed misery. It would begin with divesting myself of all designer clothes, jewelry, vehicles, smartphones and connections to fucking click-bait ecosystems. Since the tendency of humanity to sidestep immutable truth and go worship liars was the exact thing that eviscerated me in the 1960s, the last thing I was going to do now in 2019 was have anything to do with digital tech, social media or streamed cinematic art. Asking me to take a Zoom call or shop online from now on would be like asking that tiny little Jenny girl from *Forrest Gump* to go back inside that dilapidated farmhouse and put daddy's God damn dinner on the table.

⟶

Everyone in Canada of course remembers where they were the day that Jack Kennedy was assassinated in 1963 and the World Trade Center was attacked by al-Qaeda in 2001. These were events that happened in America so of course they would become the absolute obsession of we Canadians. Heck, we all still remember the day Scarlett Johansson wore the wrong shoes with the wrong outfit at the Oscars. As Leonard Cohen and I would say, this obsession with all things America is a particular Canadian failing. Anything tragic or earthshattering up here just becomes the next 6-week news cycle Macarena dance sensation, only to be expunged from the history books just as quickly as the Rideau Club culture from the center of the universe—what Peter C. Newman once called The Canadian Establishment—can get around to it.

Now all Bill Maher social-justice commentary aside, I do in fact remember where I was the exact moment when I knew I might have some form of incurable cancer. It was 11:23 p.m. on Tuesday, September 24, 2019. I had gone to bed around 9:00 p.m. feeling absolutely on top of the world. Having moved to Lower Lonsdale from that dystopian hell hole known as Victoria four months earlier, I hadn't felt this happy in a very long time. It was just so refreshing to be retired from the workforce. It felt so good to be free to do whatever I wanted with not a single financial worry in the world. Already settled into my new condo with Marianne, I was working out daily in the gym with a personal trainer and getting all my therapy sessions underway with Reilly. Free of all things digital tech, devoid of vehicles, and in open possession of a simple flip phone from the 1990s, I was pretty sure I was very close to reliving the kind of quiet serenity and therapeutic connection with nature I once felt back in 1978 in those heady City South days, and later in the 1980s in seaside Steveston. Mostly, it was just so nice to be back with Marianne, living our lives, doing our thing, laughing up a storm with all our goofy insider jokes and our bespoke idiolect that nobody listening in would ever understand. Short trips up to Whistler in rental cars and dinners out with Megan and Alena were now our two new favourite obsessions. We were back to gentle intimacy and untroubled peace, and with all of my post move-in chores out of the way, I was back to taking long slow walks with Lupin in and around our resplendent 5th and Lonsdale neighbourhood.

At 11:23 p.m. that evening all things changed. They changed dramatically. They changed forever. I was originally awakened by what I thought was a mosquito buzzing around my ear. I soon realized that it was just my imagination. I was soon overwhelmed with this unbearable sensation of nausea and light headedness. When I got up to take a pee I almost fainted on the way to the bathroom. I took some Tylenol and went back to bed hoping it would go away on its own. It didn't. It was a sensation of agonizing nausea that would stick with me 24-7 for at least 10 more months. I would often say to anyone who listened that it felt like being carsick, seasick, airsick, morning sick pregnant, hung over, and trapped in a Bare Naked Ladies concert—all at the same time. Puking constantly, I soon lost 26 lbs. on my already overly thin frame. I had no appetite and spent most days in bed or on the couch writhing in kill-me-now agony. Soon came months of shivering cold and bones that would crack like dry branches on a campfire. This was followed by eggplant purple bruises all over my body. I once scraped my shin when struggling to get to the toilet. It bled non-stop for three weeks. Unable to swallow and white as a ghost, I was soon ravaged by an endless stream of low-level infections: pink eye, ring worm, cold sores and seasonal flu. I had a constant sore throat and runny nose. For a guy who could once do the L-seat iron cross and giant swings on the rings back in high school—who could always take any wannabe tough guy straight to the mat well into his late fifties—it was just so embarrassing not being able to twist open even the simplest jar of pasta sauce. Although my bloodwork showed a plunge in all my blood panels, nobody could ever bring themselves to utter the cancer word. Initially the focus was on my heart. My ejection fraction was now down to 30 percent, and my resting heart rate could barely attain 36 beats per minute. I of course received all those inane it's-probably-nothing reassurances, but all the specialists were certain that my symptoms were merely consequences of a failing heart. Overall things looked so bad I was soon tested for HIV-AIDS. At my lowest point I looked just like Rock Hudson and Jack Layton at their two goodbye-world news conferences. Only I could make it all the way to the promised land of inner peace and celestial meaning, only to find it on fire and overrun with famine and killer locusts. I was able to keep it somewhat together emotionally until Lupin suddenly died of sarcoma cancer in January of 2020. It was like losing Frankie way back on December 28, 1960. I cried for days. Poor Marianne just didn't know what to do. It was so heartbreaking for her to watch me suffer.

After seven months of being bounced from one clinician to another, I was finally put in touch with a brilliant hematologist by the name of Dr. Kimberly Ambler. She worked at VGH and was on faculty at UBC. She was excellent. She was great. It was April 2020, and the entire planet had just been thrown into chaos by the sudden onset of the COVID-19 pandemic. One week earlier, VGH had been placed on lockdown and all surgeries and cancer treatments that weren't absolutely life and death were cancelled. Dr. Ambler was unphased. She quickly got to work analyzing my blood in great detail. To her great shock, she discovered that

I was in a full state of pancytopenia. It meant that something was terribly wrong with my bone marrow. My red blood and hemoglobin counts were far below what they should have been. My white blood counts were in total freefall. I had nearly no platelets left to stop internal bleeding. I even had something called macrocytosis, which meant that whatever red blood cells I still had left were under great stress. Burr cells were also present. It meant I was suffering from acute amenia of the highest order. She said HIV-AIDS had now been ruled out so it had to be something far more serious. She ordered an urgent bone marrow biopsy and an ultrasound of my spleen. The ultrasound showed that I had an enlarged spleen—which explained the sucking sensation I'd had in my solar plexus from as far back as September 24, 2019. The biopsy confirmed that I had a rare type of cancer known as hairy cell leukemia. It's incurable, but it usually responds well to treatment. It has only two suspected causes. It's generally felt that it's either caused by a mutated V600E gene, or as was reported in the *New York Times* in 2009, exposure to Agent Orange over in Vietnam. It's a malignancy of B-cells which work in tandem with T-cells to fight infections and enable inoculations with acquired memory whenever pathogens or vaccines are introduced to the bloodstream. Never one to be fussed by hospital lockdowns, Dr. Ambler got me booked in right away for a concentrated course of high-dose chemotherapy. It meant I had to sit in that chemo chair at the leukemia and bone marrow transplant ward for five days in a row without any pause in between. I took Metonia to keep the constant nausea in check. I was finally sent home on May 8, 2020—immunocompromised with a near-zero white blood count. It meant I was walking out into a COVID-saturated world with absolutely no means to fight off any infection—of any kind. Standing beside folks without masks felt like soaking in the bathtub while some drunk teeters close by with a plugged-in toaster. Dr. Ambler gave me instructions to quarantine at home for several weeks and to rush to the hospital the very moment I started to develop a fever of any kind. She said that any infection, no matter how small, could be fatal. I was to watch out for something called febrile neutropenia. It was something often referred to as neutropenic sepsis. I wasn't sure what was going to happen next, but I was greatly comforted by all the special care I had been given by Dr. Ambler. The medical consensus was that without her quick action, I would have died within days. There is just no way a 63-year-old recovering alcoholic with severe cardiomyopathy and a 78 percent progression case of hairy cell leukemia could have survived another week without a prompt first line chemotherapy response. None of those Vietnam vets who'd been exposed to Agent Orange in the 1960s ever really lasted more than a few months after returning home from the war. Through it all, it was never lost on me that Dr. Kimberley Ambler—just like Marianne Bianco—was born and raised in Peterborough. Just another crazy coincidence I guess for little-old Russ Grabb from sunny ways Bramalea.

It was Mother's Day, 2020. May 10, 2020, to be exact. Megan had just turned 30 years old the day before. The planet was in absolute turmoil due to the ever-exploding first wave of the COVID-19 pandemic. Just up the street from our tiny condo at 5th and Lonsdale was Lions Gate Hospital. Known as LGH by all the locals, it was in full lockdown mode due to an outbreak on one of the medicine wards wherein nine patients had just died from COVID. It was the site of the hospital morgue where Canada's very first COVID fatality victim had been taken a couple of days earlier for an autopsy following his sudden death at the local Lynn Valley Care Centre. I was comforted that I was safe at home with Marianne in triple-layered quarantine protection. I was heartened that the week before it had been Alena who drove me to and from chemo every single day. Once again I was the

Snoopy and she the Doghouse. After all the extreme nausea I had just endured for eight months, I told Dr. Ambler that I'm probably the only patient in the history of oncology to ever beg his doctor for vomit-inducing chemotherapy. I kid you not, the nausea caused by my chemo was a fraction of what I had been feeling at home in the months leading up to it. Here on Mother's Day—full irony intended—I was praying that in a matter of days it would soon go away for good. I remember thinking to myself around noon that day that surely to God it can't get any worse than this. Surely to Christ the three Goddesses of Fate had made their point. Sure, I was that fucking idiot who deserved to get his pathetic loser ass kicked for all his many transgressions—both at home and in the workplace—but come on. I was deeply sorry for everything. I was doing everything I could to fix what I broke, and to make up for all the harm I had caused on so many levels. As they used to say on the playground back in 1966, Uncle!

As the supper hour approached that fateful Mother's Day, I said to Marianne, "Can you please check my temperature? I'm feeling kind of warm, and I'm all sweaty." I assumed it was the early bowl of elbow macaroni I had just eaten, but I wanted to make sure. Sure enough the thermometer said 100°F. It was a slight fever, but no biggie. Fifteen minutes later it was 102°F. Within 30 minutes it was 104°F and I was starting to drift in and out of consciousness. I called the leukemia and bone marrow transplant ward at VGH and asked them what I should do. The nurse said, "Get your ass to LGH right away, you're in febrile neutropenia. It could be fatal." I replied, "Does that really make sense, given LGH is now the center of Canada's worst COVID outbreak?" She snapped, "Get your fucking ass over to LGH, I mean it." Getting a ride from a trusty neighbour, I was at the front steps of the ER fifteen minutes later. Marianne watched as I was ushered off in a wobbly wheelchair, slumped over like a winded ragdoll. It would be the last time she would see me for what seemed like an eternity. Once inside the ER it was all a big blur. Soon I was in an isolation room being told I had neutropenic sepsis, a faltering heart, and something very serious called an AKI. I later learned it was an acronym for acute kidney injury. Somehow I had picked up an infection while completing my chemo at VGH. I was soon being tested for COVID and something called C. difficile. What really hit home for me was when they told me my white blood count had just dropped to 0.6. I knew it should have been in the 4.0-11.0 range to give myself a fighting chance. Worst of all, my lymphocytes—the very things that one needs to fight off COVID—had also dropped to 0.1. For any mere mortal to survive even a tiny papercut, a lymphocyte score of 2.0 would be the bare minimum required. I knew I was probably done for when the Internist entered my isolation room and asked me my opinion on DNRs and whether I'd be good with intubation—if it ever came to that. As you know, DNR is hospital speak for Do Not Resuscitate Order. Citing my cardiomyopathy condition and my AKI, she said they'd do everything they could. She said she was hoping we wouldn't have to resort to dialysis, but she had the equipment at the ready if required. As they hooked me up to an IV infusion of high-dose antibiotics I looked up at my patient monitor and saw that my heartrate had dipped to 32. In addition to crippling nausea, I was soon overtaken by an endless stream of watery diarrhea. With an ejection fraction of 30 percent—and with LGH then being the very epicenter of COVID transmission across Canada—it didn't look good for a stroke survivor like me who still wasn't out of the woods yet with leukemia. I tried to reassure Marianne over my flip phone that I'd be home soon, but she just knew. She knew this could be it. Her tears flowed unabated for hours. Just like me with Alena on November 6, 2009, she was saying to herself, "How could this be? We've come so far and endured so much. Please God, please don't let him die. This is just so unfair. He's a good man. He's a good person. He's done so very much for this world. Please, please just give him one more chance. Please don't let my honey die."

———————⁓

They say that—when it comes down to this—you at some point see your entire life flash before your eyes. I had some prior experience with near death moments, so I knew it doesn't quite work that way. It was Saturday, May 16, 2020, and I had been here at LGH for seven long days: the first two spent in an isolation room down in the ER, the last five up here in 428 East, in what's known in hospital land as neutropenic quarantine. It meant I was dumped all alone in a dark room the size of a small motel suite with my own bathroom and wash station, where nobody was to enter without first donning extreme measure PPE far and away more elaborate than what's worn when dealing with COVID patients downstairs in the ICU. It meant that until my antibiotic regiment had finally brought my sepsis to heel, there was nothing anybody could do for me. I had no complaints about this arrangement. Sure, I was lonely and unable to receive visitors, but it just made good scientific sense. If even the tiniest of germ was going to kill me, then who was I to bitch about being buried alive in a tomb where no pathogen could ever get to me. Sure, nurses came in every few hours to check my vitals, empty my diarrhea-filled pan, recharge my IV bags, and bring me tiny thimbles of bland food. Sure, the phlebotomist came in once a day to draw blood. Yes, the Internist would swing by every morning to update me on my condition. But honestly, what else could anybody do? It was simply a waiting game, made tolerable only by frequent flip phone calls to Marianne and the girls at all hours of the day, and quiet contemplation about my downward spiral. I was of course comforted to learn after Day 4 of my penance that COVID-19 and C. difficile had been ruled out. I was also glad my AKI had been resolved through intensive rehydration. Whatever was eating away at me would forever remain a great mystery. I was trying not to go all drama queen here, but honestly a part of me just couldn't help but think this was probably you-know-who reaching out from the grave one last time to jolt me with all her how-dare-you loathing and self-loathing. It was a terror-soaked dance of lunacy she and I had been doing every evening in her crinoline and my short pants to the tune of *A Summer Place* by Percy Faith ever since my birth on April 2, 1957. When you fall down into this type of feces-drenched pit of nausea suffering, what else is there to think about?

***

"Fuck off, Grabb. He's never gonna talk to you. He's all lawyered up. Why don't you just go home and eat a bowl of dicks." It's what all my underlings politely had to say to me back in the summer of 1992 when I was brought in to clean up a murder case that was trending off the rails—out in Chilliwack in those heady pre-DNA days. It was just how cops spoke to each other back then. Not cops who wrote house book cards and briefing notes for the Minister. Not cops who spent months crafting business cases for helicopter purchases and strategic action plans that looked so God damn pretty when published in glossy brochure format. But you know, real cops—the kind who went 72 hours without sleep for the greater good of Canadians whenever they're called to the scene of a real crime. You know, not a crime involving the shortage of pens and scotch tape in the supply room—or an armed policy analyst with a cop uniform and a badge being forced to sit in a high-back office chair that wasn't really his or her favourite colour.

Turns out there were indeed other things for me to think about as Day 6 of my imposed misery in 428 East finally rolled around. Turns out I just couldn't stop thinking about that one case where Keith Harrison, age 45, of Calgary drowned his 7-year-old stepson Michael Kolibar in the Fraser River because the authorities back in

Alberta were getting close to uncovering the real truth about their little morning-shower and forced oral sex routine. Harrison had just been charged with second degree murder in relation to this homicide and was now in custody at the Surrey Pretrial Centre. Worried the evidence might be a bit shaky, I proposed that I go see him to ask if he might voluntarily admit to what he did. Hence all the "Fuck off, Grabb" expressions of derision and doubt. Never one to stand for any fucking animal getting away with drowning their very own son—and used to being cast as that annoying prick who just never gives up—off I went. Off I went and of course I came back six hours later with an apology letter and a signed written confession that prompted Harrison to quietly plead guilty in November of 1992.

Looking back now, I realize that I started thinking about this Harrison homicide case when I was at my very worst in hospital because it had been yet another time when confronted with the insurmountable I reverted to the kind of dig-deep will to persevere that was once taught to me by Terry Mercury out on the football field way back in 1971. The memory of a little boy being drowned by a parent also triggered a huge flow of emotion. Lying there in that soiled gurney day after day, night after night—having lost all sense of time—I knew I had to dig deep yet again, and visualize doing another 32 wind sprints even though I was completely spent. I just knew I had to reflect back on all those cases where I just wouldn't give up—no matter the cost to my health, or my good standing with my peers back at the office. Thinking about not being willing to quietly throw in the towel on Michael's murder gave me that tiny spark I needed to push on—and not die in that moment. Thinking about the fact that a full 43 years earlier I had been in the basement of this very hospital—witnessing the gruesome double autopsy of those two baby girls from Lions Bay—jarred me to fight for that next desperate breath. Day after day, night after night, I cried alone to myself in that hospital bed wondering how little Margo Lynn and Tupene Lee were doing up in heaven after having been so unspeakably burnt alive, and neglected by their very own mother. I also thought a lot about little Mary Alice Philips who in 2011, at 20, successfully sued the B.C. Government for $2.6 million for what her mother had done to her way back in 1993 in Boston Bar when she was only 2. You remember her. She was that infant who was left permanently brain damaged and blind after her skull had been cracked against a coffee table in the family home. I'm glad I'd done my part in sending her mom away to prison for 5 years. I was delighted those social workers paid dearly for their own inexcusable measure of blind-eye negligence. At the time I was relieved the Siska First Nation had pushed so hard to get justice for little Mary. But repeatedly thinking about poor Margo Lynn, Tupene Lee, and Mikey Kolibar was what kept me from going to the light. I was certain all three were up in heaven begging me to stay alive—just in case some other little boy or girl needed a caring man like me to step up and do what nobody else ever seemed willing to do. Imagine being told to just go home and eat a bowl of dicks when you're just trying to do the right thing. Imagine a world where doctors tell leukemia patients to just go home and have a nice warm bath. How about a police constable who orders a tiny little 10-year-old boy to just go home and allow his own evisceration to continue unabated so a repugnant predator and her enabler can sidestep being disgraced—so the pristine Canadian delusion might still live on. It all ended with me sobbing in the loving arms of Nurse Beryl—after she found me wandering around 428 East buck naked, desperately looking for my can opener and my 1967 railway map to Grandpa Fred's house.

So while it's all well and good to chuckle about how lived experience can sometimes play a huge serendipitous role in truly jaw-dropping outcomes, it's not always what actually makes the full difference. Are you wondering how it was that I survived such a close brush with death under such agonizing conditions—and went home to spend the next 18 months in bed writing down everything that I could ever remember about my extraordinary life before it was too late?

If you're wondering about this, I've got just one word for you:

Marianne.

Yup, earth angel Marianne.

Every morning when I peered out the window of that dark and dreary isolation room at Lions Gate Hospital I looked down four floors to the street below and saw beautiful Marianne Bianco from Peterborough sitting in a weathered lawn chair waving up at me like the Dickens. Barred from entering the hospital due to COVID protocols, she just wasn't going to be deterred from being close to her man. As she put it, nobody was going to hurt Russell Grabb ever again. She would lay down her life to save mine. Whether it was some skank charging me with a knife, or all those holdouts back east—still dismissing me as a nightwatchman with a whistle working on contract with the B.C. Government—nobody was going to fuck with me anymore. She would have none of it. She wasn't down there bathing on some roof like some hallelujah angel in some Leonard Cohen song, but when I eventually got home she sure as shit tied me to a kitchen chair and washed my hair. It took a feces and vomit-drenched trip to the doorsteps of Heaven—and all her undying love and devotion—to get me there, but I'd finally found safety and inner peace. It was late May 2020. All the streetlights were just starting to come on. I'd just turned 63 years old. Sweet mother of fucking Jesus, I'd finally made it. Depraved indifference would forever define the Canadian collective—and all those keepers of the maternal message back east would forever argue I'd never actually suffered abuse-abuse—but me, well, I was now completely free.

———————————

So, think about it.

If I had died from that frightening 1965 drowning, my very last pleasant sensation as a living, breathing human being would have been the alluring scent of all those Crayola crayons.

That candy coloured house would have been my last resting place.

If I had died from that 1979 knife attack, my very last observation as a living, breathing human being would have been that crooked tea towel hanging off the front of that filthy stove.

That white stucco walk-up would have been the place where it all ended for me.

If Alena had died in that trauma room on November 6, 2009, her very last words as a living, breathing human being would have been, "Daddy, I can't breathe. Get them to take this rubber mat off my face. Daddy please. I can't breathe. Help, please, Daddy, I can't breathe!"

An inner city hospital replete with clanging noise, horrible smells, and sobbing critical-care nurses would have been where Alena and I would have both met our maker together.

If I'd been run over by that BMW after suffering my stroke in Victoria in 2017, my very last observation as a living, breathing human being would have been the sight of that licence plate coming toward my forehead at what seemed like the speed of light.

A bustling one way street in a downtown urban setting on the doorstep of a Lululemon store would have marked the place where all my terrible suffering would have come to an end.

If I had passed away in May of 2020 due to complications from leukemia, my very last pleasant sensation as a living, breathing human being would have been the sight of Marianne sitting in that lawn chair at 13th and St. Georges mustering up every ounce of strength she had to reassure me that I mattered, that I belonged—that I was always loved for who I really was.

In the warm waiting arms of redemption and untroubled peace would have been how I would have taken my long awaited place in Heaven.

***

As I sit here now in January of 2022, sipping my morning coffee from my Elections BC mug, way out here in the grand majesty of what I still call City South, reflecting on everything that finally got me to this place of assured safety and purring kitten tranquility, I'm reminded of the lyrics of that hypnotic anthem from 1983 by The Fixx, *Saved by Zero*. It's the notion that the secret to true happiness lies in one's decision to unhinge oneself from all the cancerous trappings and adornments of social elitism, material possession, and blind compliance with imposed conformity—and to push back against evil and danger no matter the cost to one's self. It means being content with nothing other than just your inner soul and the glowing affection of those you love. I still face the stark reality that my leukemia cancer is incurable, and I'm still waiting for someone to say, "Russ, you poor bastard. Is there anything I can do?" But not lost on me is the notion that I still have Marianne, Megan and Alena. At age 31, Megan is a rising star in the business world—still on a first name basis with Judge Oppal—still sleeping at night with her trusty baby blankets. The other pigtail pretty one, Alena, at age 29 is striving for med school, but still goes by that cute little nickname, Alena Bear. Marianne still bends down to tie my shoelaces knowing that when I was a kid I never really mastered that task—knowing that I really never had any real childhood to speak of. As a loving family of four Grabbdashians, we've never been this close. Never this safe. Never this happy. I truly have been saved by zero. When you think about it, there's really not much else one ever really needs. Just the other day I asked Marianne, "Honey, have you seen my speedy getaway running shoes?" She replied, "They're in the front hall closet where you put them, you nutbar." The first and only time I'd ever truly let my guard down like this was that short period in 1978 when, at the age of 20, I'd fled Toronto and isolated myself from all the demonic clutches of my mother. I guess now I'll finally be able to answer the question Megan posed way back in Grade 3: "Dad, did Grandma hurt you?"

"This is just how an unfathomably injured child speaks."

— Russell George Grabb

Printed in the USA
CPSIA information can be obtained
at www.ICGtesting.com
LVHW092201161123
764211LV00002B/3